Notes from a Diviner

in the

Postmodern World

A Handbook for Spirit Workers

Theresa C. Dintino

Notes from a Diviner in the Postmodern World:
A Handbook for Spirit Workers
Copyright © 2016 by Theresa C. Dintino

ISBN: 978-1-939812-92-6

Cover art by Annie E. Dintino

Dedication

To the wedeme, the stick, and the spirit bell.

Contents

〜〜〜

Appendices

≈

Acknowledgments

To all of my students, for trusting me to guide you in your journeys to become diviners. I am forever grateful and appreciative for all you have taught and continue to teach me as you go on to explore these landscapes yourselves.

Many thanks to all who have come to me for divinations and allowed me to look into your worldviews and belief systems. These sessions have provided some of my most valued insights.

Gratitude to you all.

An extra special thank you to my editor, book designer, and friend, Cris Wanzer, as well as my writing buddy, Melissa Smith Baker. Working with the two of you all these years has not only enriched the writing process, but also made the intolerable places tolerable and fun! Love to you both.

Author's Notes

The articles included here as appendices were written before I became a diviner. I include them here as further reading for those who wish to delve more deeply into some of the subjects cited in the main text of the book.

As I put this book together, I realized I had included the information from Brian Swimme, Ph.D., on the development of the membrane in the early sea, in three separate places. This is obviously a very pertinent piece of information to me. You may find it repetitive, but I wanted to leave the information intact within the separate articles as they appeared, so that each piece can be read individually.

A word about the Dagara Tradition...

I have the deepest respect for the Dagara tradition of stick divination into which I am initiated. Stick divination, because it has been held for so long and so well by the Dagara people, has a potent field. Because it is an oral tradition, many people may view my writing about it as a sort of blasphemy. I have made my best attempt to be clear about which information comes from that tradition and which pieces are my own interpretations and musings. It is offered here only with the wish for greater healing in the sharing of its gifts.

Introduction

Divination is inquiry and conversation. A diviner looks into the spiritual dimensions around another person and delivers to them what they need to know according to the information the diviner is receiving. Many differing energies and entities come to speak. These can be ancestors, elements (Earth, air, fire, water), elemental beings, animal allies, elemental forces, deities, light beings, star beings, or even other parts of the person that are alive in other dimensions. A diviner interfaces with all of these. This interfacing and the rituals that arise from it are often called "medicine."

When I became a diviner, I did not expect to encounter a *landscape* in the otherworld that I would become familiar with and navigate more easily as I continued to divine. I am still exploring this landscape, but wanted to share some of the things I have learned in order to help those interested in the dimensional realms understand better what they are seeing. What I have included in this book is not meant to be rigid; it is a conversation and a guide.

I am a scholar and writer, my focus being on women's spirituality, Neolithic cultures of the Goddess, and women's history. I have a spiritual lineage in the Strega tradition through my father's family, who emigrated from Italy to New Hampshire at the turn of the last century. The Streghe, both male and female, are the medicine people, witches, and healers in Italy.

In 2011, I was initiated into the form of stick divination from the Dagara people of West Africa. One becomes a diviner in Dagara tradition through merging consciousness with an elemental being. I am merged with three wedeme (elemental beings of the wild). My journey toward becoming a diviner is more fully explored and written about in my book *The Amazon Pattern: A Message from Ancient Women Diviners of Trees and Time.* For more detailed instruction on working with the trees, read my book *Teachings From the Trees: Spiritual Mentoring from the Standing Ones.*

Stick divination pulls on everything I have ever known, learned, read, and experienced. As the wedeme work with me in the divination setting, they "mine" every part of my consciousness in their desire to communicate what they are seeing from their dimension and point of view. There is nothing that is not useful. They will pull on memories, feelings, riddles, fairy tales, movies...anything to help me understand and better communicate what they wish to say. They work tirelessly in this effort.

My work with the wedeme is what revealed to me this landscape.

We live in the postmodern world, which holds a worldview that is vastly different than the villages, belief systems, and times from where most of the divinatory practices arose. Postmodern diviners must find a way to contextualize the information in the here and now of where we live for those who come to us, all the while being mindful and respectful of the cultures that this information, protocols, and traditions came from.

With the mixing of traditions, the postmodern world has created many of its own gods, goddesses, entities, and belief systems as well. A postmodern diviner may encounter gods and goddesses of all traditions, see chakras that need healing, prescribe herbs or a visit to the allopathic doctor, prescribe rituals that include crystals and colloidal gold as well as ash and stones, encounter Jesus and Mary, vampires, werewolves, and the Anunnaki...all in the same divination!

A broad mixing happens in the divination space for a postmodern diviner that is unlike any that has existed before. This is a formidable job, and one that needs holding, training, and careful guidance.

That is why understanding the landscape can be helpful.

Divination is important and it wants to be here. Many forms of it have landed here from a variety of places, and have been met with much interest. It can bring a point of view that the postmodern world is very much in need of. It awakens our ancient and primal selves. It speaks to the hunger and vacuum created by the postmodern world itself: the longing for connection, belonging, and purpose. Divination can help restore balance to a world very much out of balance by human actions, and to people who often feel out of balance and are looking for a way to heal. As the wedeme have said, it can help us grow *from the inside out.*

This book is an effort to not only normalize divination in the postmodern world, but to help it thrive.

Chapter One

The Elements, Elemental Forces, and Elemental Beings

The elements, elemental forces, and elemental beings are a large part of many spiritual traditions. They are three different things entirely, while at the same time intricately interconnected and interwoven. They are often confused and misrepresented in language and definition; therefore, it is important to try to understand their differences in order to be more effective in our interactions with them.

It is helpful to examine the roots of the words "elemental" and "element" for a better understanding. *Elemental* means primary, basic, fundamental, root, and rudimentary. *Elements* are original and related to origin. We can think of both element and elemental as something in its pure form.

When something is elemental, it is considered essential and necessary, a basis upon which something else is built. Elements can also be considered components or parts that make up a whole. Elemental and element also imply an authentic part of something—*our elemental self;* that which we consider persistent and lasting.

What is an Element in Spiritual Cosmologies?

There are four or five elements that are considered to be the fundamental components and basis of life. They are often listed as *fire, water, air*, and *Earth*. In Chinese cosmology, we add *wood*. The Dagara medicine wheel leaves out *air* and adds in *mineral* and *nature/wild*. In some traditions, each element is equated with a direction. Each cosmology works with the elements as entities and beings with particular properties and abilities. (These elements are not to be confused with the Periodic Table of Elements that we learn about in chemistry.)

The elements are considered to be beings with distinct personalities and properties, and are treated as such in indigenous cosmologies. The water, the Earth, the air, and the fire are all alive energies that combine to create our reality. These elements are considered to be that which created life and the ones who allow life to continue. They exist in tandem with each other, separate but interconnected, and work together in concert to retain the web of life.

We need to be in balance with these elements, honor them, and understand their particular energetic properties so that we can live healthy and fulfilling lives. Medicine people help facilitate this relationship and an ongoing dialogue with these elements for the benefit of the whole. Based on their particular abilities, they are utilized for varying healing functions. It is important to become intimate with each element in order to interact with them and experience a participatory relationship with our world.

What are the Elemental Forces?

Elemental forces are energies such as rain, thunder, lightning, wind, and storms. These are often collectively called *weather*. They can also manifest as floods, volcanic eruptions, earthquakes, and tornadoes. These are presentations of fire, water, air, Earth, and other elements that are unpredictable and fierce, often harbingers of extreme change ushering in crisis and ultimately restoring balance. In many cultures, these potent forces are anthropomorphized as Goddesses, Gods, and mythological creatures as a way to further interact with their power and unpredictability.

Elemental forces and the stories that have constellated around them remind humans of their own limitations and powerlessness in the face of these entities. A humble respect is needed when dealing with the elemental forces. These forces are also often viewed as powers humans need to be in balance with in order to live noble lives. In their mythological and anthropomorphized forms they are often viewed as the Keepers of Balance, and are portrayed as such: Thunder Beings, Archangels, Cosmic Justice, Egyptian Ma'at, Greek Zeus, Norse Thor, and the like.

Humans can embody these forces both unconsciously and consciously. Many traditions believe that embodying them in states of ritual trance and dance is an effective way of being in relationship and communion with them. By forming and maintaining a relationship with them, medicine people can listen for when things are out of balance and ask what is needed to help set them right.

Elemental Beings

The elemental beings are the small beings who live in the different spheres of the Earth, and are deeply connected to the primordial Earth. Elemental beings are the children of the unions of elements or elemental forces and places/locations on the Earth. That is why the elemental beings often have local

3

qualities and can manifest differently in different places.[1]

Medicine people and elemental beings have long been friends and have collaborated together to bring healing and blessings to the Earth community. The elemental beings know place and location well, and are in deep resonance with the elements and elemental forces. They can lead us back to these elemental relationships and our elemental selves.

Chapter Two

The Wedeme: The Elemental Beings of the Land and Wild

I n the Dagara tradition from West Africa, the wedeme (*oudeme*) are the elemental beings who are the *keepers of the wild*. What could this possibly mean? To better understand this, it is useful to examine closely the words *wild* and *keeper*.

Wild

In this tradition there are five elements: fire, water, mineral, Earth, and nature/wild.

Wildness is the potentiality of the life force. Wildness is that which sustains life.

Wild is what *might* happen.

Wild is untamed, undomesticated.

Wild is virgin; untouched, unharmed.

Wild is free.

Wild is pure. Pristine. Innocent.

Wild is fierce. Wild is unknown.

Source Energy is Wild

The term "virgin wildness" has been used by the wedeme. These are not my words. According to the wedeme, wildness is purity. The Source Energy of the origin of the Universe is wild. "Sweeping" (cleansing) rituals are often prescribed in divination to remove psychic "dirt" and *return people to their original blueprint,*[2] but it is more accurate to say that these rituals return them to their own wildness, or Original Source. Original Source is wild. Whatever you conceive Source to be (Goddess, God, the One, the All, the Universe), to be disconnected from our own wildness disconnects us from Source. The wedeme are the *keepers* of the wild. They remember Source. To make pure, to return to a virgin state, is to return to our own wildness.

The Call and the Response

The wild is the fertile potential created by the call and response; the meeting of the two that creates the three. Wildness is birthed in the interaction between the creator and the created. The unexpected, unanticipated, unimagined that continuously births potentiality — this is the wild.

In this way Source and Origin are ever new, because they are truly wild.

Land Elementals

The wedeme are also known as the elemental beings of the land, as opposed to the elemental beings of the water (*kontomble*). They live on and in the land, and are born from the meeting of Earth and other large elemental forces. They are *keepers* of the wild places, the wild animals — the four-legged, the wild grasses, the wild underground, and inner Earth.

Keeper

The wedeme are *keepers* of the wild. What does it mean to be a *keeper?*

To *keep* is to continue *having or holding something*, to *maintain a relationship to*, to *be faithful to*, to stay *in accord with*.

In the Dagara tradition, a term often used is *sob*. Those who tend to and *keep* the relationship with the kontomble (also the broad word for elemental beings, which includes the wedeme) are kontomble*sob*. The keeper of the Earth Shrine (*Tengan*) is the Tengan*sob*. The keeper of the sacrificial knife (*suo*) is suo*sob*. *Sob* is commonly translated as "owner of," but a better translation is indeed *keeper*, one who maintains a right relationship with, one who *tends to*. These *sobs* are *keepers* of the medicine, *keepers* of these particular shrines and practices, *keepers* of the relationship with these beings, and entities for the good of the community.

Sob is also translated as *priest*. A priest is again a *keeper*. One who *priests* or *priestesses* a tradition is *keeper* of that which they priest; one who tends to it, listens, responds, and holds it for others.

Wedeme are *Keepers* of the Wild

The wedeme are in reciprocal relationship to the wild. They are *intimate* with it. They *keep* the wild alive and whole.

This is incredibly interesting and intriguing. How do these beings possibly *keep* the wild? These must be magical creatures indeed. I don't know that we can ever understand how the wedeme do this, but I am ever in awe at the magnificent choreography of a Universe that creates *keepers* of its own wild potentiality to ensure continued birthing of the new.

And we humans get to interact with these beings! No

wonder this relationship is called *magic,* and that they appear in our stories and mythology as just that—magical and enchanting beings that can take many forms and grant our wishes.

The wedeme are the tricky and loving pranksters. Playful, they love to laugh and giggle, and delight in making us laugh. Our laughter is food for them. The wedeme craft witty and brilliant jokes. They play with our languages and words. They create riddles, and want to "puzzle" us. Because of this, they can appear childlike in their innocence and presentation, though they are ancient and wise.

Their relationship to the wild may be one of the reasons why they have also been so maligned, and are often feared and accused of evil doing. Though they are small, this is a huge power they hold, and a huge responsibility. They must be true to the wild. No matter how domesticated we humans try to become, they will *keep* the wild.

Keeping a Relationship to the *Keepers* of the Wild

Humans who are in relationship with the wedeme are *keepers of the keepers* of the wild. This is a very important commitment, to tend to those that *keep* the wild, and attend to the *keepers* of the potentiality of life. As a diviner, much of this tending is done through shrines created for them, as well as ritual and divination. This is how we listen to them and all they have to say, how we attend to them, offering them sustenance from our dimension and deep friendship in the shared heartspace.

The wedeme are also sovereign beings with free will and choice, and must be respected as such.

You do not have to be an initiated diviner to be in relationship with the wedeme. Entering into a relationship with one is not a small commitment, but you will not be punished if you do not "do it right." Like any relationship, you get out of it what you put into it. Relationships grow and thrive and have a wildness of their own that needs to be tended to and *kept*.

Your relationship with your wedeme will mirror your relationships with other beings and humans in your lives. This is simply an interdimensional affair. You can learn a lot if you are willing to go the distance with these wise and magical beings. The "payoff" far exceeds any "cost" on your part.

Go to the wild places and listen to what they have to say. Examine your own relationship to the wild, both internally and externally. If you decide you wish to know them, begin by carrying that simple prayer in your heart.

Divination is Listening to the Inner Voice of the Universe

The inner voice. The small voice we often do not listen to. It is not a small voice at all, but one that is more subtle, and therefore difficult to hear in our busy lives full of louder, less important voices, like the list of things to do, what others have said to us, or what we are taught is the truth.

The smaller, more subtle *inner voice* is often our authentic truth that gets drowned out by these louder and less important voices. Part of the reason why one goes to divination is to make time to listen to the more subtle voices — the voices from other dimensions, the voices of the unseen who are always with us but get talked over. The wedeme have a small, subtle voice. They are also able to hear the voices of the other realms and dimensions.

When one is merged (initiated) as a stick diviner in the Dagara tradition, they are able to make space for the wedeme to come inside them, literally. Inside the darkness of the

9

diviner's body, the wedeme are able to listen to the *inner voice of the Universe* and communicate that to the diviner. The *inner voice of the Universe* includes the voices of all the subtle realms. The diviner listens to the wedeme inside them and translates this information for the client who has come for divination.

The technology of getting our bodies ready for this dynamic interfacing is what one goes through on their way to becoming a diviner. The wedeme lead the initiate on a journey to heal and open their bodies — all bodies, gross and subtle — to be able to hold this other entity inside them long enough to listen and deliver the information they are receiving.

I see this interfacing as a molecular and atomic restructuring that happens. Once the person is able to open this gate for others, he or she divines by listening with all parts of their body. The information comes through the lens of the physical apertures of the diviner, which is much broader than what we think of as the five senses. Each diviner learns how to listen to the language of the elemental beings he or she is in deep relationship with. This is a technology that is familiar and known to humans, as they have engaged in it for millennia.

Taking the time to listen once again to the subtle, *inner voices* of the Universe — including our own — is essential at this place of paradigm shift in which we currently find ourselves.

The Wedeme Asked Me to Deliver These Messages

The wedeme is the term for elemental beings of the wild or land in the Dagara tradition. These beings have many names in many cultures and manifest differently in each, but they serve the same function and seem to share the same concerns in spite of human constructed cultural divides.

Working with the wedeme is not always easy. They can seem to want a lot from us...countless offerings, rituals, and lots of jewelry. It can feel like a lot of work; work many people don't understand why they should have to do. When these conversations arise, my common response is, "As far as I am concerned, they are so darn cute, they can have whatever they want."

But the truth goes much deeper than that. The wedeme are so steadfast and ardent in their commitment to the Earth and the human heart, all and any effort I can make in my human life pales in comparison, and is but a tiny drop in the ocean of work they are doing on behalf of us and Gaia. If they ask for a ring or a necklace of mine, or food or some vodka; if they tell me to go to the water and offer some milk, I give it gladly. They don't want it for themselves. There is another person, place, or entity that needs it for healing and they can deliver it there. Their comprehension of what is needed where on the Earth in a certain place and at a certain time so far exceeds mine that I no longer question it. "What?" I respond. "You need this piece of metal I have been wearing around my neck for four months, or this ring that my mother gave me on my wedding night? You need some of this food, or vodka? Here you go, you little cuties. May it serve its future purpose well."

The truth is, I will do anything for them. Therefore, if they want a few pages to speak directly to you, they can have them.

You may find this crazy or see it as a giving up of my power or sovereignty to an interdimensional being, but I know that it is not. Until you sit in divination space for hour upon hour with these beings, feeling how much they want to help the person sitting across from you and how hard they work to try to do that, it indeed may not be possible to understand. But trust me when I tell you there are beings on this planet far more evolved than humans and the elemental beings are among their ranks.

Message From the Wedeme: Let's Dance and Play Once Again

The wedeme want me to talk to you about them. They want to come back into our lives and hearts. They want us to believe in them, believe that they are alive, that they are real, that they are here on Earth with us. She is our shared home.

The wedeme love us. They care about our hearts. They feel our pain deeply. It is not exactly compassion; rather, it is empathy and concern. They feel they can help us. They want to make us strong; strong in the way a plant can be strong, firmly rooted and grounded in its place, trusting in the sun and the soil and the cycles of life on this planet.

They want us to have more iron. "Be fuerte," they say. Be solid and grounded in and with each other. They are reaching their arms out to us. "Take our hands," they say. "Let's dance and play once again together, out in the glades and forest groves, drinking in the morning dew and praying together to the stars. There is so much joy here in this place of togetherness," they say. "Together we can win."

It has been very difficult for them to be separated from us. They have waited for us to remember them, to be able to see them again and welcome them again. They have been very lonely for us. Forming a relationship with them is a huge gift to their world. It offers them so much light and warmth—a soft, yellow lovelight.

The wedeme are the eyes and ears of the Earth, Gaia's little helpers. They were here long before us, born of the union of two or more elemental forces. They are elemental—wild and original beings.

They love and admire us. They admire our hands—these hands that can make things, like rings; things they can adore and admire. They admire our handwork; the ability to string together grass to make a broom, or reeds to make a fence.

They teach us these skills. They learn them by living in the deep inner Earth where Gaia does these things inside her body. They are gifters of skills and crafts: smithing, forging, planting, harvesting, fermentation and beer making, and divination. They show us how to smelt as she smelts the ores inside herself. As she combines elements and chemicals within her, they teach us how to do it with our hands on the surface, giving us recipes for healing potions. We surface creatures can use Gaia's inner skills to further create, as she does deep in the Earth. They can communicate this to us. That is why relationships with them have always and can once again be truly collaborative.

They know how to make things grow. They want to help us grow and stand tall. "Fuerte. Strong." They make things grow in the inner Earth; they make trees and plants grow tall. They hear us breathing. They want us to breathe more. "Minerals for strength," they say.

They guard the crystals that grow deep in the Earth. They help them grow. They nurture and protect them. They see how they grow. They observe the same crystals in our bodies and endocrine glands, and want to teach us how to help them grow and stay strong.

They remember life inside the stars. "We forged the elements in the stars," they say, "and now forge minerals in Earth. We love metal. We love your mettle. We want to give you more to help the Earth grow and expand beyond the bounds of her current limitations, *from the inside out*," they say. "Let us help you grow *from the inside out*."

Message from the Wedeme: The Trees are Our Friends

The wedeme want you to know you can talk to them through the trees. Like the roots, the wedeme can carry things between trees. "You think you invented the Internet?" they ask. "Where do you think you got the idea? But ours is the intra- and extra-net. We deliver messages within the Earth as well as outside of our home planet."

The human heart is the surprise in the Universe. Potentialities are aimed at and ideas are seeded from the vast cosmic mind, but surprises are always happening. This is wild potentiality. Who knew that when the stars and their light carriers had the idea for humans, the human heart would be the surprise? The wedeme say: "We are in awe of your hearts. They are an almost impossible development. Appreciate this gift inside your body. Your heart has many etheric bodies as well. Spend as much time getting these muscles fit and healthy as you do other muscles in your body, and you will live in a different reality. What exercises and meditations do your hearts need in order to grow and reach their full potentiality?

"Some of you have become so obsessed with psychic phenomena and the evolution of your pineal glands that you are not paying attention to this gem inside your chests. It doesn't matter what you know. It matters what you feel. Some of you already understand this. The purpose of physical embodiment is to move information streamed from light through matter. The human heart can *feel* the light. This is the surprise development.

"Share this heart-transmuted light with the trees today. We will carry it where it needs to go."

Message from the Wedeme: Heal the *Cracks* in Your Hearts

The wedeme very often focus on what I call "heart healings" in divinations. They seem to be masters of this art and offer a lot of their energy to this. I have long been impressed and have wondered over this.

Recently, in a divination the wedeme explained to me that one of the reasons they are so focused on our hearts and heart healings is because the "cracks" in our hearts are the places that allow us to hurt others. These cracks in our hearts are mirrored in the interior of the Earth. Where we hurt, She hurts. They are also what allow us to hurt and do damage to the Earth.

When we are mean or cruel to one another, this emerges from the wounds in our hearts. This is very difficult for the wedeme. It hurts them deeply when we are hurting. They feel it in their bodies and the body of the Earth, and don't know how to help us. However, by healing the cracks in our hearts, the places inside us scarred from previous wounding, they can help us not to hurt others and perpetuate further hurt. And that is why they are so committed to healing our hearts. If they can heal our hearts, there is less chance we will hurt the hearts of others, and that makes the Earth a safer place for them.

Our own wounds, if not tended to, can allow us to wound others. Healing our hearts, they said, does not only heal us, it prevents us from spreading hurt further, and heals the Earth as well.

For me, this is an important teaching. We are at a crucial place in our evolution as a species. This kind of thinking requires us to take radical responsibility for our own actions. Can we examine the places inside ourselves that are wounded and allow us to wound others?

We must look at these places with compassion and

kindness, and ask ourselves to clean them up. The cycle of pain will not end unless we do so. As long as we are in pain and carry that pain around with us, we are a danger to others. We are sensitive beings who can be easily hurt, but when we allow our wounds to fester and go unhealed, we are not taking responsibility for the pain we may cause others.

Chapter Three

The Earth Shrine, Tengan/Tembalo, and the Hallow

The All-Important Earth Shrine

I n the second divination I ever received, I was told my grandmother on my Italian side, who had passed years before, was sad. The diviner received information that there was something my grandmother had not done. She felt badly about this and hoped I could pick it up again and repair it. I was not told what she had not done. To begin the journey to repair this, I was given a ritual to do for her, and was encouraged to ask more about what she needed.

When I performed the ritual for her, I was shown the image of what she called an "Earth Shrine" that she had neglected. My grandmother's mother was a Strega—a wise woman in the Italian tradition—who immigrated to New Hampshire in 1900 and struggled to keep the ways of her medicine tradition in this new place. Her daughter, my grandmother, had not carried on the lineage. She wanted to integrate into the American culture she was born into, and what she viewed as the "old fashioned" Strega ways were not part of that. Though her mother had asked her to tend to this shrine after she passed, my grandmother had not done it.

The neglected Earth Shrine that I saw was a place in the forest that had clearly once been an active shrine. Now abandoned, it was covered and overgrown with brambles. The shrine was in the middle of a grove of trees, and made of various organic materials with a geometric form in the center of it, on the Earth. I could see in this image that many offerings had once been made in this place. I could also see that this shrine was suffering from years of neglect. The sadness I felt when I was shown this image I assumed was my grandmother's. This is what she had not done and was asking me to pick up again and repair. This was part of the tear in the fabric of the lineage she had created by her refusal to carry it forward, and the subsequent neglect of all its components.

With the feeling of sadness came the understanding that, for various reasons, my grandmother had simply not been able to see to this task in her lifetime. Now on the other side, she was able to see the gravity of her decision and she was asking me to help her fix it. Compassion for her moved through my body. I loved my grandmother so much, of course I would help heal this on my side so she could find deeper peace on hers. I made the offering I had been instructed to make for her and pledged to help repair this.

Though I willingly made this pledge and commitment, I did not know where to begin. I no longer lived in the place in New Hampshire where I had grown up and where this shrine had been, and where it might possibly still be. The lineage had been broken and lost in my family with my grandmother's refusal to hold it and appropriately pass it on. I had very few tools in my kit at this time to fully understand this. I trusted I would be taught what this all meant in time.

The divination this information came through on was the second one in my journey toward becoming initiated as a diviner in the West African Dagara tradition. When I returned to the person who had carried out the divination—my original mentor in this tradition—his simple response was that "only men are keepers of the Earth Shrine in the Dagara tradition." He had never heard of a woman doing it.

At the time, I did not know what an Earth Shrine was, or that they even existed in the Dagara tradition. I was intrigued to learn that there actually was such a thing in the Dagara cosmology, and the Italian as well. The fact that my mentor dismissed me by saying it was a role reserved only for men meant nothing to me. Men had usurped women's roles in every tradition. Why would this one be any different? Since I had seen that my grandmother and my great-grandmother were keepers of the Earth Shrine, I knew that women clearly held this role in my own personal lineage, and more than likely women once held it in the Dagara tradition. The remark "only men can do it" is never revelatory of any deep truth. Rather, it simply reveals the patriarchal fingerprints that are on a tradition. I would rely on my female mentors on the other side to show me how to pick this role back up when the time was right.

Now, six years later, I have a much greater understanding of the Earth Shrine and how it is vital to keeping the medicine alive. The Earth Shrine is part of a "pattern of wholeness" that is embedded in all Earth medicine traditions, though perhaps articulated differently in each culture. The all-important Earth Shrine maintains the web of networks and connections that keep an alive tradition nourished and fostered, and allows the medicine to grow and thrive in its own time and place. A healthy and well-tended Earth Shrine is essential for any medicine work.

Tengan/Tembalo

In the Dagara tradition, the Earth Shrine is the Tengan/Tembalo Shrine. Classically, Tengan (what it gets abbreviated down to) is seen as the male Earth and Tembalo as female Earth. The Tengan Shrines have jurisdiction over a certain land area/geography. The Tengan Shrine is tended by a Tengansob (keeper of the Tengan Shrine) and oversees all Earth/land related activities in the jurisdiction of said Tengan Shrine. The Tengan Shrine, in its indigenous context, sees to issues of agriculture—planting, harvesting—as well as marriages, births, burials, relocation of homes, and moving of shrines, and changes within the area it "governs." It oversees the integrated reality of the spiritual as well as everyday aspects of village life.

Offerings are made to the Earth (Teng) at the Tengan Shrine as well as anywhere on the Earth to Tembalo through a "nipple" created with a clump of earth. The Tengan Shrine is typically stones and/or a tree. The tree shrine periodically requires sweeping (ritual purification), especially if some infraction has happened to the Earth or if a murder or suicide has occurred within the land that is overseen by the particular Tengan Shrine. The Tengan Shrine is also the place where land and other disputes within the community can be settled through divination by the Tengansob. The Tengan Shrine has an important place in village life and the medicine.[3]

What the Stick Said

My colleagues and I carried out a divination to learn more about Tengan/Tembalo, and how we are to carry forward and maintain this prototype in the place where we live with our local medicine community. We were given a beautiful image of a meeting of Earth and sky facilitated by the Tengan tree *(Tengan tie)*. The divination showed how this activated configuration holds the medicine in a certain location upon the Earth.

There appeared a very large white bird, or "angelic" winged creature who stretched her wings over the circumference of the Earth. The energetic arc of her wings was mirrored in the Earth below her, far below Earth's surface, to form a lenticular shape. The horizon or surface of the Earth was the midpoint of the meeting of these two, arced energetic boundaries. The Tengan tree was the "pole" between them. The Tengan Shrine held the meeting of Earth and sky and created the place within which the medicine could thrive. We were told this meeting of Earth and sky creates a magnetized field, which is the medicine. The human and other beings who inhabit this area created within this pod-like circumference can participate with the medicine in the designated and tended space governed and held by the Earth Shrine.

It is as though an etheric "tent" is created by this Earth Shrine structure. Within it is an active and contained space. The Tengan bird spread her wings like a large umbrella, encompassing an area of the local ecosystem in which to house and augment Earth medicine.

"Tengan holds up the sky," the wedeme kept saying. They warned us not to get caught up in gendered language. "Rather, see it as a meeting of Earth and sky." This tent-like formation creates a microcosm, the inside space alive with an energetic, swirling, white light. From this image it was clear that the Tengan/Tembalo Shrine creates a container for the medicine. It creates a permeable membrane.

Cosmologist Brian Swimme cites the emergence of the membrane as one of the most crucial developments for the presence of life on Earth.[4] Swimme describes the existence of molecules in the early sea; how in the early Earth system, complexity is created and then washed away by the ongoing forces of nature. But there is a "moment where a molecular web folds around a complex chemical interaction and that molecular web protects what has been developed." This is the birth of the cell. All other life forms emerged as a result of this moment of creativity. Membranes also possess the power of *discernment*, deciding what to allow in and what to keep out for the overall integrity of the cell. Swimme calls this a form of intelligence and notes that human sensitivity is yet another variety of this development created by cells in the early sea.[5] "The membrane protects complexity and creative power."

I see the medicine pod created by the Earth Shrine as but another manifestation of the membrane forming around that which has been created to preserve and protect it, like a mother's arms.

The medicine is alive. It needs healthy, permeable membranes created and held by activated and tended-to Earth Shrines to keep it healthy and thriving.

In that divination on Tengan/Tembalo, I saw the Tengan Shrine as tended to by a council of humans rather than one person. I was shown how the Tengan tree can feel the vibrations of events in this field as they emanate through the telluric realm and sense thought forms, dreams, and desires in the atmosphere of the above portion. The above and below communicate in a constant feedback loop through the tree shrine.

The Tengan holds this pod-like space for a village or medicine community to exist within. In our context here in North America, it holds the pod within which the medicine can thrive. Land use and planting rights are not relevant for us here.

Other Tengan tents or pods appeared across the landscape

and were shown connecting to one another. Some were smaller satellites (*Tengani-le*) of the larger Tengan Shrine, housing smaller areas within the larger sphere of influence. The Tengan Shrines fractalized out in such a way that created a larger and more robust circumference with each activated shrine. The more there were, the stronger the medicine was. Medicine people were responsible for happenings and healings in their Tengan's sphere of influence. Through interactions and connections with other Tengan locations and the medicine people held in the jurisdiction of other Tengan pods, medicine people were interactive with other loci for the medicine. This way, a medicine person handles their own area in a manageable way, while maintaining a connection and offering healing in other places held under the jurisdiction of the other's Tengan Shrine. These pod-like containers create concentrated areas that can overlap and intersect.

Stick divination, facilitated by the wedeme (elemental beings of the wild) for the humans, is held within this pod-like context. Each stick of every individual stick diviner is a fractal of the Tengan, bearing healing properties and holding the medicine within their Tengan's diameter. Many diviners call upon and answer to one Tengan Shrine, and there are smaller ones as well that they can tend to at their more local level. Therefore, one diviner can be held under and by many interacting and overlapping Tengan Shrines. All beings held within this space benefit from this magnetized energy. Plants grow better and communities thrive.

This was a beautiful cosmology I was shown. Within the pod-like space, the energy was charged, fecund, and potent. I began to believe this is possibly what many of the ancient sacred places were/are on the Earth. Churches, temples, mosques, and other places of worship came to hold a similar function in later times. But this picture was more inclusive.

This was a picture of humans, elements, elemental beings, elemental forces, animals, and beings in other dimensions all meeting within this beautifully magnetically charged area to participate with Earth medicine for the further evolution of life.

The Hallow

So, where does all this fit with the Italian cosmology?

Before I learned about the abandoned Earth Shrine in my lineage, the Dagara Earth Shrines, and Earth Shrines as commonly held by trees, I had been led by my great-grandmother in the beyond to begin to work with the trees. Through her guidance, I developed relationships with what began to appear to be a network of trees. All had different medicinal qualities and characters, and were holding different functions in the place they inhabited on the Earth. All held strongly the connection between Earth and sky. Different celestial energies and beings could be accessed through each different tree. Some were in local parks, some on mountains, some by rivers. The circumference of this network gradually broadened as my great-grandmother and the trees led me to more and varied locations.

Then there were the teachings of the groves. It is important to remember that all trees once lived in groves, though this is hard for us to imagine now, in our urban, suburban, and even more rural lifestyles where we have left some, or many times only one tree standing between the structures we have built and inhabit. Trees are community beings.

There was one particular Bay grove that I had been led to on a local mountain that helped me remember that trees do not exist in isolation when they are allowed to express their organic orientation. In the time that I knew this grove, I had been asked and taught how to activate it. I had met the angel/bird presence connected to it, and the grove itself had become a source of power for me.

I met this grove quite by accident, while out on the mountain one day. There was an eerie feeling to it and I was not sure I should enter it. That night I was awakened from slumber to find the grove itself in my bedroom asking me to return. In that nighttime visitation, what felt like a female bird or Goddess-like being appeared inside the grove. She had the presence of white light and seemed to be some sort of celestial energy related to the grove itself. She was cloaked and mysterious. She assured me it was safe to return. She wanted to be reactivated and worked with again in this grove. This grove emanated power from deep below the surface of the Earth and seemed to have a center place for the power that wished to be worked with once again with this female light being.

I did not understand the visitation or the request, but I did return to the grove later in the week to make offerings and listen. The grove and the mountain together were offering to be a source of power for our local medicine community to draw on. The grove was presenting itself to us as a place to work and to carry out rituals.

Through a series of visits and divinations carried out in the grove, following the lead and guidance of the trees and this celestial being in this grove, I was taught how to activate it. The grove, though a collection of many separate trees, had what felt like a group mind. There was a oneness to the trees there. The grove itself was a being with consciousness. At this time I learned that the Italian name for grove, *boschetto*, was the same as the word for coven. This was stunning to me. I began to understand that groves of trees were covens, and explored all the associations this potent information carried. The grove told me the women were not the covens, the trees were. The women went to the covens of trees and received their power from and through them. Groups of women working in covens were groups of women associated with groups of trees.

The word "covenant" and its origins are interesting to bring in here. A covenant is an agreement, a contract—a pledge. The trees being called covens expressed a sense of commitment to one another, a pledge and undertaking of a contractual agreement through time.

In subsequent divinations for others, and in further workings with groves of trees, I have come to see how groves of trees hold a special function on the Earth and in the greater cosmos. These groves seem to be entities or group souls that stay connected, though they may have been cut down in their 3D form. I have seen how groves of trees seem to arise from a spirit template beyond the Earth plane, meaning groves of trees seem to be an archetypal energy that exist beyond their presentation on Earth. They remember each other and stay connected in the ancestral and other realms as powerful entities. They want to be remembered and worked with again. They indeed do seem to hold a sort of covenant or agreement that goes beyond their Earthly embodiment.

In another piece of work I did with a colleague in a cut-down redwood grove, I was shown how the groves, when actively worked with on the European continent by the medicine keepers, each had their own tone. Together, when they were all active, they formed a sort of "pipe organ" function on the Earth. This pipe organ kept the energy field toned, but also sent songs and messages out from the Earth to the larger solar system and cosmos. Perhaps these celestial beings/angels/white-winged ones each carry a celestial tone that the grove, through time, becomes attuned to.

I am sure there is more to discover, but groves of trees calling themselves covens began to appear and speak to me in many places. Deforestation began to feel more sinister than I had ever imagined it to be. The magical forests and groves of ancient stories and fairy tales began to take on a deeper meaning. The groves held a power and a template on Earth mirroring a template in the greater cosmos that had been decommissioned, perhaps deliberately, and was wishing to speak to us once again.

This is not to say that all groves are Earth Shrines. Certainly, some serve other functions, and some are simply groves. In order for a grove or tree to function as an Earth Shrine, it needs to be installed and activated with a certain protocol by medicine keepers. There needs to be an agreed upon, intentional collaboration from the trees, the humans, and elemental beings of the place at the very least.

Perhaps originally Earth Shrines were held by groves. Perhaps this more ancient template was what I had been shown in the image of the abandoned Earth Shrine in my own lineage of birth. Perhaps in our state of modern deforestation, it has come to often be held by a single tree. The groves taught me that they can hold the medicine in a similar way as the Earth Shrine, Tengan/Tembalo Shrines.

The grove seemed more resonant to what I had been shown as my Italian lineage's Earth Shrine. I was fascinated to later find this passage in a book by the Stregone Raven Grimassi.

> Witches of the Old Ways draw power from the Hallow. This is a term for the deep center of the forest where primal sacredness exists. From this center, power emanates outward to the three realms: above, below and in-between. Power also flows into the Hallow from these realms as well. For modern practitioners this is a concept rather than an area in an actual forest, but the ancient practice of venerating a specific tree in a

sacred grove is connected to the theme of the Hallow.[6]

Now I saw, years after I had seen my grandmother's abandoned Earth Shrine, that I was being organically taught about Earth Shrines and tending to them through the trees and groves themselves.

In the center of my grandmother's abandoned Earth Shrine was a mandala on the Earth. It seemed to be a portal connecting to another grove in Italy that had been physically left behind when my family emigrated. But nothing is left behind etherically. It was quite possible that this ancient Earth Shrine in Italy was still available to me in energetic form in the ancestral realm and beyond. Now was the time for me to find out, and perhaps reopen the portal to the Earth Shrine waiting for me there.

Chapter Four

Fire and Ancestors

Original Fire and Cosmic Source Entities

irst there was fire: Original Source. We all came from this fire. Fire is first. This Original Fire is still here. It never went away. We must stay connected to this Source Fire. It is what feeds us. When we "die"—are ready to transform, morph—we return to it.

As I moved along in my work as researcher, scholar, and stick diviner in the Dagara tradition, I noticed a prefix in many of the entities' names; the prefix Ny. It seemed that this prefix referred to Original Fire and the Cosmic Entities that support and are most closely associated with She that gave birth to the all, the primal womb fires—Source.

Below are a few of these entities.

Nyame

According to the research of Eva Meyerowitz, to the Akan of Ghana (a neighboring peoples to the Dagara) Nyame is the Supreme Goddess that gave birth to the cosmos.[7] She split herself into three parts: Cosmic, Earth, and Underworld. Nyame is the eternal fire, the one with no beginning and no end. Her fires burn on. She births all and sustains all. Her element is gold. Precious and rare, gold on Earth is Nyame.

The community tends their connection to Nyame through a shrine called "Nyame-dua" (Nyame's tree). This shrine is a three-pronged tree branch. A bowl of water rests within the branches. Nyame deposits Her Fire into the water of this cauldron, enlivening it for the well-being of the community. Community members dip their hands into the water to thank and praise Nyame, and to have her praise them. It is a reciprocal offering. One is praised when one praises. One is cared for when one cares for.

One can reconnect herself to Nyame, Source, Original Fire, by tying a white string to the shrine or onto a tree which represents her. Often a fig tree is identified as the "Gya-dua," Nyame's fire tree. The fruit of the fig is representational of Nyame's nurturing womb space.

Nya-Zièlé and Nyur

In Dagara belief there is Nya-Zièlé, "she who brightens the cosmos."[8] Again, Original Fire.

And there is Nyur: soul rootedness. The Nyur Shrine of the Dagara has the same form as the Nyame-dua Shrine of the Akan: a three-pronged branch with a bowl of water on top.

Community members are held in rootedness through the Nyur Shrine. Medicine circles are joined and held together through the interwoven and underground roots of many individual and family Nyur Shrines. The medicine is held strong through this Nyur Shrine network.

While like Nyame-dua and Nyame, Nyur roots Nya-Zièlé's Fire on Earth, from a prescriptive point of view, when Nyur comes up in divination, the focus is more on roots and rooting, grounding and holding one's soul essence (the spark of

Original Source within us) firmly and securely into this Earth-body experience. Nyur is about issues of belonging and knowing one's place in community. The word *nyogfu* means *attaching to and belonging to*.[9] Whereas Nyame-dua is concerned with connection to Source, Nyur deals with issues of connectedness on the Earth plane. Being grounded, centered, and strongly rooted in one's life, family, community, and soul purpose is healthy soul rootedness.

Community members dip their hands into the Nyur water, humbly wash their faces with its medicinal tincture, or make offerings into it when they have lost their orientation and sense of belonging on the soul level.

Nyamping

The Nyamping in the Dagara tradition are often referred to as "the old, old ones—the ones that are so old, no one remembers their names."[10]

I later learned that the Nyamping are also the ones who come to get you when you die.[11] I was familiar with this concept through my Italian grandmother, who could always name who had come to collect a family or community member when they died. Beings come for you when you die to escort you back to Source. This is one function of the Nyamping. In the Strega tradition, these are the Lasa.

I went on to learn more about the Nyamping on my own with those I divined for and with. Here are some of the things we have learned:

The Nyamping are closest to the fires of Source; of Nyame, of Nya-Zièlé. The Nyamping are the keepers of the fires, the fires of Nyame. They are the transitional gate holders. They examine the preparedness of the one making the transition. They stand at the transitional thresholds.

If you push your way through, it will not be good. There has to be readiness on both sides. This readiness the Nyamping watch and guard for. When the time is right, they lead you through the fire.

Dragons and Nyamping

We were also told that Dragons are Nyamping; they are one and the same. Dragons and Nyamping are engaged in birthing consciousness; the consciousness of the original Genetrix.

Dragons exist in all realms to hold the consciousness of the Nyamping, keepers of the fire, in all realms. Dragons are a "spark" of this Original Fire. Therefore, dragons are in all the elements (fire, water, Earth, mountain, wild). Our soul/consciousness is also a spark of this Original Fire. Each of us is associated with a certain element, and that is where this dragon (spark) lives within us.

Feeding Original Fire

If we want to continue to be fed by it, we need to feed Source Fire. There is currently a great neglect in feeding this ancient fire. We need to tend to the keepers of the Original Fire by feeding them and the fire.

If you are a woman who is still bleeding, please make an offering of your moontime blood. This is Nyame's Fire within women. Also, if you are of childbearing age, you can offer your child's placenta to the Nyamping (Lasa) to honor these fire creators.

Other offerings that can be made to Original Fire are: high-quality, edible vegetable oil of any kind; oil with hibiscus juice in it; or crushed dandelion greens in oil. Please use a stone or wooden mortar and pestle to crush your greens. Do not use metal. Make these offerings to the Nyamping at the base of a tree for the eternal fires of Source. It will be much appreciated.

Why Ancestor Work is Important

The Ancestors are associated with the element of fire in Dagara tradition. We are birthed out of the fire and return to the fire when we die. One who makes his or her safe return to the fires of source upon death has become an ancestor.

The ancestors are a major part of divination work. This can be perplexing for some who have no relationship with their ancestors, and downright disturbing for those who feel they do not like their ancestors.

The way I like to look at it is: an ancestor is anything that has given birth to us in some way and therefore continues to be an evolving part of us. Yes, the stars are our ancestors, bacteria are our ancestors, and humans too are our ancestors, even if we prefer that were not the case.

At this time on the planet, we all have a lot of ancestors.

We continue to learn after death. And we continue to change after death.

The importance of ancestral work stems from the belief that, in general, it is good and wise to remember and honor those who came before us. After all, we would not be here without them.

The ancestors never really leave us, and given their different perspective in the ancestral realm, the ancestors know things we do not. They can help us if we are willing to listen. In fact, they *want* to help us.

Working with the ancestors does not mean you have to like or agree with their choices. It does not mean you are condoning behavior that they may have perpetuated in their lifetime that you feel was not upright and kind. But it does mean you understand that you have a responsibility to them, as they do to you, because you are descended in some way from them.

Many people say, "We can't choose our families." Well, then you can't choose your ancestors either. Many other people say, "You chose your family very deliberately." Either way, choice or not, we are stuck with our families and our ancestors.

Being the human who is currently embodied in 3D form and has ties to those who came before us, as well as obligations to those who will follow us, means we are in a crucial position. The choice we make to either help heal our ancestral line, or not, is an important one.

Indigenous belief states that anything that is not working properly in the lines of your ancestors will continue to affect those who come after. This includes you and your offspring. If you are in a position to help this, which you are as the one who is currently embodied, why wouldn't you? Of course, you may choose to do whatever you wish, but to me it is a win/win.

If you are too angry and resentful to help them, then you are passing that work on to your children or your children's children. If you choose not to have children to get out of this, it will simply move to someone else in your line: niece, nephew, cousins, and so on.

You cannot escape it.

We all came from somewhere and someone. We all came from those who came before us. None of us were plopped here without any lineage. We may want to believe we arrived here from another planet or by accident. We may say over and over that we do not belong here, but it is not true. If you are here, you belong here. And all humans born on Earth were born out of a female body. That female body was birthed out of another female body and so on and so on....

If you are adopted, you simply have more ancestors to deal

34

with. Nothing gets you out of it.

The ironic, but perhaps comforting part is that many of the troublesome ancestors can become our biggest allies. Since they are the ones who need the most help, they tend to show up in divinations most frequently. However, one of the cosmic rules seems to be if you help someone or something heal on the other side or in another dimension, they often become an ally you can then call on when you need help here.

This can apply to places you help heal as well—mountains, waterways, places in the Earth—what you help, helps you. Healings enable healing. It is also true that anything you heal in yourself, you may then offer as healing to another.

Some of us have fabulous ancestors. I have plenty, which I am grateful for. But I also have some who perpetuated much pain in their lifetimes through ill-chosen actions and decisions, or the unconscious acting-out of their pain.

It is true that most of us have both kinds. And most of us will become both kinds. Being human is tough and we all make mistakes. That is why ancestor work is so very important. You may need help too, when the time comes for you to be an ancestor. Bet you never thought of it that way.

Yes, there may be events in your ancestral line that need remediation. You may be called on to lend a hand with this. But know that facilitating this is not that difficult, and will help you and your descendents. You may feel that your ancestors are lost to you. This can be very unsettling. But *they* have never lost you. Getting back in touch with them can help you live a more fulfilling life.

Inquiries into Fire and Ash

The following two excerpts are from group theme divinations on fire and ash, carried out by me and a close circle

35

of colleagues. It is what the ancestors, wedeme, and elemental forces spoke to us when we came with the inquiry. In theme divinations, though the diviner holding the stick is doing the main listening and translating, everyone in the room is actively involved in the process as well. This is a group, collaborative effort that pulls on the collective field of wisdom in the room. I share it here in the spirit of generosity and abundance.

Fire is a Multiplicity of Beings

There is celebration and excitement from fire. It loves to be invited and related to. It needs something to play with, like a host, to ignite. Fire is longing to be played with more. Currently, it is seen as utilitarian. It is objectified. It would love to play and dance with us. We have stopped talking to it as a being. It has gotten a bad rap in a lot of worldviews (e.g., "the fires of hell"). People often associate it with evil.

Fire wants to be treated with respect. When you add a new log to the fire, place it lovingly. Don't throw it in. Remember, you are feeding the fire. It is alive. Think of what you would do with a person's mouth. You wouldn't shove the food in.

Though the word seems singular, fire is a multiplicity of beings. Many things come together to create fire. That includes the host that ignites and what later feeds the fire. Fire is the creator being, specific to the creation of matter. Fire is an alchemist. There is an interaction, the coming together of more than one thing to create friction. There is heat that gets created when two things rub. The two or more meeting is the meeting place that is called Fire. This is on many levels.

"Inspiration" is a form of fire where one thought meets another, or *sparks* – to spark something. The fires of creativity are a celebration; a beautiful reunion of friends with the touch and the dancing and the playing again is a form of fire. Within a fire, the wood and the fire and other elements being burned may all play together once again.

Within a fire, the particles are released from a "stuck" form, i.e., released from being "wood" or "tree" or "paper" or whatever else we may offer to the fire to burn. They are released back into their pure form and can become part of the primal creativity again. Fire is useful for rituals that require release.

There is a celebratory nature of fire, and this is part of it; the celebration of release and freedom, and the return to the field of potentiality. All the fractal levels of reality resonate with a fire on Earth, in harmonics, as when stars are born. Every fire is a memory of the inside of a star, the birth of a star. Imagine all that gets forged and reforged in fire!

Ancient people knew how to talk to fire. It's why flames were called tongues. They would ask questions of it. Then they would feed something to the fire and watch for a response. This is fire divination.

There is a way that fire likes to be invoked that is useful before starting a fire.

Fire within

Fire without

Fire come and light this fire

Perhaps you would like to begin welcoming fire in this way.

The Ancestors are Ash

Many people who believe in reincarnation find themselves confused as to how one can be an ancestor and a reincarnated human at the same time.

I found this to be a very good question, and an even more interesting question when people began to show up as their own ancestors in the divination space. *If this person is sitting right in front of me and also showing up as this being in the beyond, who is also them, then what am I actually being shown here?* I wondered.

In a stick divination, asking to learn about fire, and why in the Dagara tradition ash is the ancestors, we were told that ash is *that which remains* after a fire. Ash is *that which remains* after all other parts of a fire are burned off, released to become something other, to have further experiences and embodiments. An ancestor is the same. Ash is the ancestors and the ancestors are the ash because they are both *that which remains*.

Fire is a process that burns off and releases all it can of a community of beings back to the Source field to have further experiences. For example, the trees, the paper, the molecular structure, and combination of matter and forces that came together to make the tree into what we call *wood* get released from these bonds, these agreements that create *wood,* and are sent back to the Source field of potentiality to become something new; to have new relationships, new experiences, new bonds and agreements. Some would also interpret this as new lifetimes.

What remains after the fire is that which remains from all of these relationship agreements; experiences that cannot be burned. Ash. Ash is that which cannot be burned. It remains. This is also what the ancestor is. That which remains of all the experience—possibly what we might call the "eternal."

In that moment, I understood how we can be ancestor and a "living/embodied being" simultaneously, or how an ancestor can be an ancestor while also reincarnated as another being. The part that is the ancestor is like the ash of the fire, and the part that has become something other is the part that got released by the fire back to the particle level to meet up with other particles and continue on in a new iteration.

"Ancestralization" — the ritual through which an embodied being who has died is returned to the ancestral realm — is the process of the element of fire "burning off," either literally or metaphorically, all that can be released from the physical entity, leaving behind what remains: the ancestor/ash.

Chapter Five

Being a Healthy Diviner

D ivination is a time out of ordinary reality to interact with and listen to beings in other dimensions. Since this is a rare occurrence to many of us in the West, there are many common misconceptions. Divination directly accesses ancestors, spirits, elemental beings, and more. We are lucky to have this opportunity, but it is not a time for the diviner to surrender her own power and will. The divinatory process is participatory and collaborative. To learn more about divination in general, see my book *The Amazon Pattern: A Message from Ancient Women Diviners of Trees and Time.*

In a divination, the diviner is not only interacting with and listening to beings in other dimensions, she is translating and delivering that information to another human. Some of the information can be quite difficult to understand and translate, and even more difficult to deliver. This is when the human diviner needs to be in command of herself and the space.

The diviner must be comfortable holding boundaries, speaking her voice, and not allowing unresolved personal issues to get in the way. It is important to be a conscious, healthy human to be a helpful diviner.

Common Misconceptions

Don't Leave Your Power and Voice Behind When You Divine

Many people think they lose or cannot assert their power when dealing with beings in other dimensions. This is not true. You do not lose your power, will, or voice while having a spiritual interaction, nor do you lose your boundaries, or you could really get into trouble. Take your brain, your common sense, and your discernment with you; otherwise, guess what? You won't have them. Common sense and spiritual realities are not mutually exclusive. If you are a mature adult, you are a human being in control of your life in all circumstances. Why would you think or act otherwise in spiritual interactions?

If you have issues with boundaries in the 3D reality, you should clean this up before delving into any deep spiritual work, or it will show up there, too. You need to be able to assert yourself. Don't relinquish your voice to interdimensional beings.

What does having your voice mean? It means knowing how you feel in any given moment and being able to articulate that clearly and nonviolently. If you cannot do this in your everyday life, then you won't be able to when working with beings in other dimensions. What if they ask you to do something you are not comfortable with? Will you agree? This is not good in any dimension.

Being Spiritual Does Not Excuse Poor Interpersonal Behavior

Hurtful behavior, neglect, or poor interpersonal manners

cannot be blamed on the fact that you are spiritual or in touch with spiritual forces. Too many people try to blame or brush irresponsible behavior under the shamanic carpet. You are responsible for your behavior and your treatment of others. Your personal conduct is your personal conduct, not the fault of your spiritual work. If you are not in control of your emotions, find a good therapist and learn some skills. Your clients do not need to hold your personal issues. Don't ask them to. If you make a mistake, take a deep breath, apologize, and endeavor to fix the behavior pattern in yourself. Step back a bit and find your center.

If a spiritual practitioner is exhibiting behavior that is unkind or abusive, and blaming it on energies beyond her control, this is a red flag. Just because you are in touch with powerful spiritual energies does not give you license to treat other humans with disrespect. Everyone is always accountable for his or her actions. No one is exempt. Many of us have "gifts" of clairvoyance and more, but how we behave in the world is equally as important.

Examine your relationships and your own inner wounds. These are your issues to deal with. They don't get a pass because you consider yourself "gifted," or because you are stressed and believe yourself to be "under psychic attack." Own your behavior and your conduct if you want to be a skillful diviner.

Commanding the Space in a Divination

The first and most important skill one must have as a diviner is knowing how to hold space. This means sealing off a location and field within which to work, stating your intentions clearly, calling in your allies and guides, and staying in your body so you can recognize energies that are not your own.

When these energies show up, greet them and ask them why they have come, all the while understanding that you and the person sitting across from you have free will and choice and are not at their mercy. Listen to what they have to say, but do not lose your discernment and common sense. It is not appropriate to say, "That is what they are saying. We must do as they say." Diviners are human beings facilitating an interaction. It is not a time to be egoic and defensive. Allow yourself to be human.

If something is questionable or does not make sense, get out of your own way and try to arrive at a deeper understanding. Make sure you understand what you are saying and agreeing to, and if you don't, then say, "I don't fully understand this, but this is what they are saying."

This is what I mean by the divination space being a collaborative and participatory one. Questioning more deeply within the realm of divination opens doors long closed and brings understanding and healing. We must give ourselves permission to question the information that is coming through by staying fully grounded in our own power.

Deliver the information clearly to the client and make sure there is consent. "This is what they are saying. Are you comfortable with this?" Or "Are you willing to do this?"

Listen to the response. Some will say no, or exhibit confusion. Good for them. They are staying in their own power. Take the time to honor their response. If they say no, they are not giving consent to continue. Ask why and let the energy of that "no" or the confusion be in the space. Often this is a healing in itself. Life is complex. Energy patterns are complex. If an unweaving of a pattern is trying to happen, let it unravel slowly. As the diviner, re-articulate what the client has said into the space. "She is not comfortable and here is why. Do you hear this?" The spirits will come back with another response. But if the diviner is not in command of the space, and gets flustered or triggered by the other person having their voice, or does not even want to hear their voice, then the divination will stay at the more surface level and be less effective.

Difficult feelings will come up that you, the diviner, will need to hold, welcome, and allow. You will be asked to sit with these and let the client work through these without being reactive or controlling. Many people have never been allowed, or have never allowed themselves, to be in touch with their feelings. At times you might have to feel exactly what they are feeling. This is very challenging, yet can be a healing moment. The energy is finally allowed to flow through both you and your client, and perhaps transform. Offer yourself as the vehicle for this transformation. Be patient. Wait until they have fully moved the energy through their body before continuing. This is one of the gifts of divination. It moves and clears energies that have been stuck in all dimensions. Don't underestimate this part of divination. Many diviners think they have to pronounce deep wisdom. It is equally important to honor energetic shifts. When it feels right, ask the client if they are ready to continue with the divination. A deeper healing is now in effect.

When difficult energies and feelings arise, and you feel stuck as the diviner and are unsure how to proceed, take the time to ask, "Who can help with this?" Most often someone will show up: an ancestor, an angel, a spirit animal, or an elemental being. They have been waiting and watching over the person. Often the client will know them. But if you don't create the space and you don't ask, this will never happen.

If people bring up subjects you are not comfortable looking at, you can say that as well. "I am not the right person for this line of questioning. I am sure you can find someone else better suited. I prefer to move on to the next question."

If you, the diviner, get confused or lost, as you surely will now and then, it is your responsibility to bring yourself back to center and re-ground into your body. You will get led into "rabbit holes" you never before imagined. This is normal. You are not doing anything wrong. Divination is not a performance and it is not a formula. It is a free-flowing, interactive experience. If you get lost, it is you who have gotten lost. Take ownership of this and work to clear your own confusion. It is not the spirits who are confused. You can make an appeal to your guides by saying, "I don't fully hear what you are saying. Can you be more clear?" Go back to where the inquiry began, before you became confused, and listen again, slowly and clearly moving through the subject at hand.

All of the above is what I mean by commanding the space in the divination. This is not a passive job. The diviner is an active participant. Don't believe other diviners who say, "It's not me. It's them." It's both. Yes, the healing is carried out by beings in other dimensions, the information is coming from them, and the diviner's chief job is to listen; but the skill of the diviner to command the space creates not only a good, but an effective, divination.

Sorcery: The Misuse of the Medicine

The Earth has had enough of the war vibration.

Last May, I was awakened in middle of the night by the grandmothers, a group of fierce, disembodied women I work with. Much to my surprise, when they awakened me, they said, "Now you must pledge to use no sorcery."

"Sorcery?" I said to them. "I never use sorcery. I only use the medicine for the greater good. I never have and never will use the medicine to intentionally hurt anyone."

45

They said, "Whether you are attacking someone or defending yourself from attack, you are involved with sorcery. Sorcery is engaging with the war vibration on the energetic level, and defending yourself is also that vibration."

"But I have to be able to defend myself from attack," I said.

"No," they said. "For a medicine person to be afraid of another medicine person is the worst thing ever. This is the worst thing that has happened on this planet. This has to stop now."

"The worst thing *ever?*" I replied. "Worse than all the other horrible things that have taken place on this planet? Could this be true?"

"Yes," they said. "If you reflect on it, you will see this is the worst thing ever. And it needs to stop."

"But how can I be safe if I do not defend and protect myself?" I asked. "That seems rather unwise."

In my training, I was taught that as a medicine person I would be attacked on the energetic level, and I must be on constant guard for this. This was taught to me by humans with good, albeit misguided, intentions. Now I was being told to unlearn this information because it was causing me to engage with what the grandmothers call the "war vibration."

Though I trusted the grandmothers more than any other, I could not understand what they were saying and I felt confused. The planet was a battle zone, and they were asking me to be here with no arsenal. Was this even possible? This was uncharted territory for me, but I knew there must be a truth here.

"We will teach you," they said, "but first you must pledge to no longer use sorcery."

"Of course I will," I promised, though I could not believe I was being accused of such a thing.

"No good can ever come of engaging with the war

vibration," they said. "It only leads to the need for more — more tools, more arsenal, more defense — and cultivates deeper paranoia. You will feel in your body when you are engaging with the war vibration," they said. "Start to pay attention and when you feel it, ask us what to do."

A short while after I made my pledge to them, I sensed negative energy coming toward me. In the past at times like these, I carried out actions to protect and defend, spreading ash at my boundaries and performing rituals to keep this energy out. But I had agreed to no sorcery. "What do I do now?" I asked them. "Now that this energy is here? Can I not seal off my boundaries?"

"No," they said. "The action of locking out is the war vibration. You may seal off sacred space for ritual and to create a container to hold the medicine for healing, but not to keep 'enemies' out. No more fortressing. Now when you feel energy of the unfriendly kind coming toward you, you ask, *What needs healing here?* and go from there to find out what to do to heal this energy, this negative vibration."

That was the beginning of the teaching. I felt this shift in my body. It was a subtle shift, but one that made all the difference because I was no longer acting from a defensive posture. I now understood them and saw that they were correct.

Here are some of the things I have learned so far in this teaching:

Move to the Position of Objectivity

The Earth is asking for an end to the war vibration. As medicine people, we must commit to cleaning this war vibration out of the medicine of the Earth. How do we engage with the war vibration? I never thought that defending myself from psychic attack was engaging in the war vibration, but now I understand that it is. Defense of oneself spiritually is part of the war vibration.

Rather than be on the defense or offense, the position to hold is objectivity. Look at the energy that is present with objectivity. Hold the objectivity with love. Love is the antidote. Rise up out of being on the offensive or defensive to be able to embrace both out of love. Objectivity should not be confused with detachment or not caring.

Being objective is to care for all.[12]

Refuse to Believe in the Normalization of Sorcery

In many spiritual circles, defense of oneself is now accepted as normal. Accepting that one is vulnerable to attack is a given. Sorcery is normalized. This is not normal.

As the grandmothers said to me, medicine people should not be afraid of other medicine people. "For a medicine person to be afraid of another medicine person is the worst thing ever." And now I see this is the truth. This was part of what happened to the medicine when it became compromised in times of persecution. Medicine people are supposed to be healers and in service to healing. To hold this war vibration as normal to the medicine is a tragedy indeed.

If sorcery is normalized in a working group of medicine people, this is indicative that things are out of balance and need healing. The purpose of the medicine is to restore harmony, not to be engaged in constant defense, and the building of weapons, stronger rituals, and potions to stave off negative energy. This is taking up precious use of the medicine and the energy of the elemental beings. This is misuse of the medicine.

What is the War Vibration?

This is a very important teaching, as most of us on this planet are completely inculcated into the war vibration. It is completely normalized in us. And I do not mean only war on the global and interpersonal scale, but the war vibration within ourselves. Competition and jealousy are very strong vibrations of war. Competition for resources, for attention and power, out of fear and "not enoughness" — these are all the war vibration.

Though I acknowledge that there are indeed negative energies all around that demand my attention, if I choose to engage with them with the frequency of the war vibration, then I am absolutely collaborating with them. I am, in fact, agreeing to engage in war with them. There is another way. The Earth is asking us to remember another way.

Know the Difference Between Conflict and the War Vibration

Conflict is not the war vibration. Conflict is normal. The way we deal with conflict lets us know whether or not we are engaged with the war vibration. If we approach conflict with wonder and a desire for healing and understanding, that is not the war vibration. If we approach conflict with defense or offense, we are engaging the war vibration.

Conflict is when two energies meet that appear inharmonious. How do we bring harmony to these two or more seemingly opposing forces? By listening to what they each have to say, being curious for what it is they want to teach us. We should ask: *Why have they come?* Banishing, abolishing, cutting someone out, withholding, sealing off, demonizing, needing to be right — these are all the war vibration.

This can be very subtle. We each need to do our own work to feel these subtleties and to be honest with ourselves about which vibration we are engaging. However, a word of warning: the war vibration can be very seductive. It allows us to engage in blame and not take responsibility for our own part in conflict. It allows us to not own the warring going on inside ourselves. It creates a feeling of entitlement and justification for our own bad behaviors. And it can tend to get us the results we have been taught to desire: power over, material gain, adoration from others, and endless egoic massage. Dangerously addictive.

To make sure we are not engaging the war vibration, we must always ask: *What needs healing here?*

Seeing the War Vibration for What It Is

Groups or individuals that engage with the war vibration require domination. This does not allow all voices or new energies to be welcomed. Those engaged with the war vibration are interested in keeping what they have acquired for themselves and a select few. The select few are those who will also protect and defend what has been acquired. Because actions can be interpreted as out of synch with the dominant party, one can be ousted at any point. With groups and individuals that engage the war vibration, there is never any true security or safety. Everyone is a potential enemy. Though we have become accustomed to seeing this behavior as normal, it is not.

All wars are resource wars. This is true on the spiritual plane as well.

No one person or group holds the blame here, but it is time for us all to take a hard look at this and agree to clean it up. If we are true medicine people, then healing is where our interests lie. As with anything else, we begin by first healing the war vibration in ourselves.

Bringing Healing to "Evil" and "Possession"

One of the more challenging aspects to being a medicine person in the postmodern world is encountering unpleasant energies, or what is often called the "shadow side of spirituality." "Possession" and "evil" are part of this.

For me it is important to always hold the question, "What is trying to be healed here?" when we consider these more difficult occurrences. This can help us stay in alignment with the true purpose and focus of the medicine: returning beings to their authentic center by restoring balance.

On a very basic level, possession is when the energy we often label as "evil" finds a home inside a human or place/space and begins to use that human or place's energy to stay alive.

Here are a few of the things I have learned about possession and evil:

Knowing What is Alive and What is Not Alive

The Earth says humans have checked out fully what it means to be evil and the consequences of that. We can choose to move on now. Are we ready to accept this? This means we no longer need to engage this energy we call evil. Is there a way we have become addicted to that?

The wedeme warn us to not focus on where this evil originated and who caused it; rather, we should focus on how to move forward into healing. Focusing on where it originated or whodunit is, in part, feeding the evil.

They say the more important issue is that we (humans) have forgotten the difference between what is alive and what is not alive. Earth is alive. Humans, animals, plants, bacteria, and fungi are alive. Stars and planets are alive. Beings in other dimensions are alive. The medicine is alive. Even Time is alive. We live in an alive cosmos.

What Does it Mean to Be Alive?

If something is alive, it changes. If something is alive, it responds sensitively to what is present, not automatically to what is expected. This is how you can tell if something or someone is alive. We call things dead that are not dead (ancestors are not dead) and act as though machines are alive (machines are not alive). Computers are machines. This is not to demonize technology, but the elemental beings are asking us to look at what receives our life energy and what does not, and understand the difference.

We forget that those whom we interact with on our devices are alive—the human pushing the keys on the other end; the one we may be choosing to send nasty messages to. That person is alive and has feelings. The keyboard you typed the note on does not. It sounds silly, but we are confused and easily led into behaviors that are not life promoting and sustaining.

It is important to give life energy to that which is alive and supports life, otherwise life is not getting our energy. And life needs energy to continue. Life is flow. Giving our energy to things that are not alive stops this flow.

It's not only technology. Many jobs, relationships, and activities can be dead-ended and therefore deadening, literally. Try to spend a bit of your time every day with that which is alive and nourishing and sustaining of life. You may be surprised by what will be revealed.

Be mindful of how you use technology. Try to look honestly at where your energy is going. What or who you are really spending it on or selling it to?

It's All Energy

Everything is energy. Einstein let us know that. That is what E=mc² is all about. We can anthropomorphize energies all we want (demons, devils, angels, reptiles, aliens, gods and goddesses), and of course we do, and we must to some degree to make sense of our realities and to "organize" our existence into meaningful categories and subject lines. Humans are embodied and we have brains that love to do this, and need to do this to live oriented in 3D reality. But the truth is everything is energy, including evil.

Energies that are fed, that receive our energy, become stronger and eventually begin to have a life of their own. We further enliven them with our attention. We empower certain energies with our active engagement and participation. That is why it is important to examine who or what is receiving our energy.

We recognize energy as "evil" when it is not life sustaining and life nourishing, creates a block in flow, leads to a dead end, and feeds only itself.

But...where did evil originate?

I cannot say where evil first originated, but I can say that I have witnessed much of what we label "evil" as having originated from infractions to the Earth.

Clear-cutting, unconscious mining, drilling, cutting into, pounding on — anything that happens that leaves a vacuum or a scar on Earth both physically and etherically, and is not consciously cleaned up or attended to — can create disembodied energies (the energy of anger, upset, disturbance, violation, displacement) that have no place to go, and therefore look for somewhere or someone to inhabit.

53

If these energies succeed in latching on to a human, this can show up as the energy of violation and abuse that becomes a repeating pattern in a family line. As this affliction moves through the generations, it can evolve into addiction, mental illness, and severe dissociative behavior in descendents.

Places that frequently experience the energy of violation that is not cleaned up can hold trauma patterns that are easily repeated at that particular location. The original violation to the Earth and life forms can turn into impulses for war, genocide, and holocaust in the human arena.

War, genocide, and the like, create more evil in that they generate further unmetabolized and disembodied energies. Not properly taking care of those who have died violent deaths (which one cannot do in a war situation) can create evil (the energy of unrest, stuckness, unfinished business, disorientation, and grief).

This is extremely complex. Each case takes careful listening to and the skillful unwinding of the patterns until the root issue is healed. BUT, the original infraction is forgetting that Earth herself is alive. If we are going to take something from her, or put something into her, we have to ask permission. The way to NOT create a vacuum to begin with is to give some energy back in return.

For millennia, humans understood these basic laws of the Universe: the law of cause and effect, the law of give and take, the law of action and reaction. You cannot take without giving back. If you use energy, you must replace it...or else it will find a way to replace itself.

This applies to the "cosmic" level of reality as well (other dimensions and the areas beyond the Earth realm), which is also alive. Cosmic energies/entities/phenomena can and do appear to us in many forms and shapes, and even have personalities. In this arena too we must give if we take, if we ask, if we seek; this is what offerings and rituals are all about. We must respect a "no" if we hear one. We must understand the consequences of our actions if we ignore the "no" and take anyway.

Most humans have slipped into a state of forgetting about this. It can seem odd or foreign to think this way now, but most indigenous cultures live this way still.

We must stop thinking of evil as something happening to us or outside of us. In truth, most of it is energy we (humans) have given birth to through our own actions. Perhaps once we truly did not understand the consequences. But if we do now, then we must act accordingly. Being mindful in our varied relationships can help us stop creating more energies that grow into what we call and experience as evil.

The Very Good News

Here is the good news: the energy we call evil is also alive. Evil is not dead. It is, in fact, an energy that has been fed a lot and is now very much alive.

Since this energy we call evil is alive, it too can change. We can help it change by offering it transformation through ritual. We can do this by asking it what it needs when it shows up, then offering that to it from our hearts with the clear and clean intention for healing and the highest good for all concerned.

This energy also needs a place to go, to be at home, to be at rest. After we have offered it healing, we must identify this, then send it there. Again, this is all done through careful listening and responding; meeting these energies we call evil with an alive response and asking our allies in the other dimensions to help us. We must come back into healthy relationship with these energies and begin to restore balance to the Earth.

If you encounter that which feels evil, don't panic. Tell it who you are, who your allies are, what you believe in, that you are on the side of life; and then do what you must to listen to it, transform it, and heal it.

Chapter Six

Water

Your Local Waters

One can tell much about an ecosystem by looking at the local water. Water holds information about the health of the local lifesystems. As a medicine person of your local place, getting to know and learning to listen to your local waters are important parts of the work.

Getting to know your local water sources is cultivating a deep relationship with the wellspring of life where you live. Make yourself familiar with your local watershed. This is the water source for your immediate environment. If you do not know it, this can be easily located by putting the name of your town and watershed into a search engine.

Different bodies of water have unique energetic properties.

River

A river is flow — movement, throughway, power line — a sort of energetic highway. Rivers are the "veins" of the Earth. The bottoms of rivers are important too. The movement of the soil by the rivers and what that creates is crucial to the life that lives there, both physically and energetically. Allowing rivers to have their natural flow and movement is essential. Rivers are related to sustenance and Earth fertility. Go to rivers when you or an issue needs flow or movement.

Streams are smaller, more localized rivers; movement and flow on a smaller scale.

Ocean

Ocean is womb, first and foremost, and the most cosmic of all waters. Oceans are more formidable than rivers. The birther of all, the ocean is the vast, powerful Mother. Shells hold the memory of the water. Shells are the concretized form of the movement of energetic and actual water; therefore, they can serve as a remote shrine for all water. When you need help or healing on a large scale, go to the ocean.

Lakes, ponds, and other smaller "contained" bodies of water

Contained bodies of water differ greatly from the above three. Their "containment" makes them unique cauldrons for healing. Go to contained bodies of water when you need to cultivate inner stillness.

Thermal/hot springs

These are places for healing and worship of deep Earth. Hot springs are places where we can be released from toxins, both physical and emotional, and require processing of our inner waters through the heat of the inner Earth.

Begin to locate, know, and understand the different personalities of your local waterways by going to them and quietly listening.

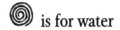 is for water

If we listened, water would teach us a lot about ourselves, our planet, and the Universe itself. If we listened, we would hear the voice of the ultimate spoken clearly and eloquently through water. If we decide to listen, it should be soon, since we are rapidly changing the qualities of this life-giving element—water.

At a Bioneers conference in Marin County, California, I attended the lecture "Waterworld: The Patterns of Nature" given by Jennifer Greene of Maine. She spoke of the positive qualities of water from an anthroposophical point of view, emphasizing that to become effective stewards of water we must understand its true nature.

The nature of water is movement. The movement of healthy water has formative capacities. Three of the forms that the movement of water repeatedly gives rise to are the meander, the sphere, and the spiral. Greene asks the question: Are these forms portraying the character of water, or are they evidence of archetypal forms in the universe working on water?

Meander: If left alone, a body of water will meander. Water not only wants to meander, but must. Through its circulating, wavy, serpentine movement (flow), water keeps itself alive. Water is alive. It is a living organism continuously engaged in organizing, creating, and sustaining itself. Bodies of water such as rivers, streams, and ponds are one single, interconnected organism, which will therefore respond to changes made anywhere upon them. Water movement and water quality are found to be in direct correlation.

Sphere: Water always strives to create a sphere. The teardrop shape ubiquitous on Earth is the imperfect form of the sphere created by the effect of gravity; however, water always strives to be spherical.

Spiral: Water creates within itself spirals, which often develop into vortices. Within moving and flowing water is water that is spiraling and spinning. Water moves in "trains of vortices, streams moving within streams...ripples."[13]

Greene's remarks about water closely paralleled discoveries I had made in my own research into ancient civilizations, African rock art, Amerindian symbols, and indeed, the recurring spherical, meandering, and spiraling patterns found over and over again in the large-scale structure of the universe itself.

For eight years I had been researching the civilizations of Old Europe, trying to understand the worldview of the people who created and inhabited villages on the Danube (6000-3500 BCE), throughout Anatolia (7000-5500 BCE), in what is now the Ukraine and Poland (6000-3500 BCE), in Greece and the island of Crete (3000-1300 BCE), and the builders of the great stone circles of Britain (4500-3000 BCE). The remains of these communities indicate a people who succeeded in living together in harmony, sharing resources, and respecting the land and the beings they shared it with. What was different? What allowed this way of being able to prosper and flourish? Imagine living in such a place!

On the archaeological remains unearthed from these cultures are many symbols. Painted onto their pottery, incised onto the walls of their dwellings, chiseled onto local rock faces and standing stones, these markings reveal themselves openly, yet remain mysterious in their meaning, becoming codes to decipher. Marija Gimbutas's irreplaceable research provides an in-depth and exhaustive cataloging of these symbols throughout several volumes of work. She viewed them as a language centered around the spiritual beliefs of the people who created them; a pre-hieroglyphic script. While compiling the information, she drew on ancient myth, folklore, and continuous tradition to deepen the text.

Within this language of symbols, or *the language with no words,* are found the meander, the sphere, and the omnipresent spiral. These repeating symbols are found not only throughout European cultures, but also in African rock art, Amerindian art, Australian aboriginal art, and art the world over. Do these symbols have similar meanings throughout these dissimilar cultures? How is it that disparate cultures with no known interaction consistently engaged similar symbols?

Gimbutas believed that many of the symbols recurring in the art of Old Europe were used to express the creative aspect of the divine experienced as female — the Goddess. The Goddess's ability to continuously create and sustain life, Her generative and regenerative aspects, were recognized and worshiped. She also associated some of these symbols with water. Of the meander she wrote, "the meandering snake and continuous meander first appeared in the art of the Upper Paleolithic. From the very beginning the meander was not used merely decoratively; it was a symbol, a metaphor for water."[14]

The word *meander* is derived from a river of the same name found in Asia Minor, well known for its striking "rhythmical loops."[15] In Modern English vernacular, it is used to indicate such a movement — a wavering, rhythmical wandering, a making up of one's way as one goes along. Drawing up silt from its bottom a little at a time, a river will meander, creating new boundaries for itself, moving itself along with its own natural flow, which is continuously changing according to the conditions it meets.

It is not only rivers, but also streams and ponds — any body of water — that must have a movement, a flow in order to be healthy. In this flowing, rhythmical pattern of movement, the water is able to maintain health as well as revitalize itself. This wisdom informs the design of Flowforms. Flowforms are sculptures, fountains, designed to move water in ways that mimic its own natural flow, forcing water through meandering spherical and spiralform shapes. The installation of Flowforms in polluted and troubled bodies of water has initiated purification and jump-started their natural capacity for regeneration.

The need for movement, flow, is true not only for bodies of water, but for all of life. We now understand that life requires an energy flow. Something that is alive creates and consumes energy in a flowing, moving, rhythmical way. Flow. Everything must flow, move, turn, change, dig the silt up from its depths, and recreate itself in each and every moment. In *Earthdance*, Elisabet Sahtouris emphasizes that a "live planet needs not only a great deal of energy but also flowing matter such as atmospheric gases and water to move things about."[16]

Jennifer Greene showed us, using her *drop picture method*, what simple detergent does to water. The water without detergent, when dropped onto a slide, displays a beautifully radiating and emanating circular design, while the one polluted with detergent remains flat, dull, uneventful, with no energetic tendril, no intricate design. It has lost its form-producing capacities.

Dams stop the natural flow of a river, forcing it into a straightened pattern. Currently dams, diversions, or canals fragment 60 percent of the world's largest 227 rivers.[17]

Theodore Schwenk, precursor to Jennifer Greene and author of *Sensitive Chaos,* laments, "A straightened river looks lifeless and dreary. It indicates the inner landscape in human souls that no longer know how to move with the rhythms of nature."[18]

~ = flow

Planets, seeds, eggs—the sphere as a symbol or a form is present everywhere. Traditionally, spheres are symbols of unity, interconnectedness, depictions of wholeness. Interesting to me are the spherical forms humans have created through the ages to serve as ritual space.

Throughout Europe we find the repeating occurrence of stone circles, especially concentrated in the British Isles where over 900 remain. Often comprised of hundreds of stones, these temples took generations to create. Many of them consist of concentric circles; a circle within a circle within a circle. The outer circle was often an earthen hill, with a neighboring, parallel ditch. The inmost circle was the **Center**, the Holy of Holies, and was reserved for ritual use.

During ritual, community members would participate with the powers of the Universe. To interact with and possibly transmute these transcendent energies, it was more effective to have them contained within this space, spherical in form. The created and bordered-off spherical form possessed the ability to assist or direct the influence these powers had over the physical world. The circle served as a container within which these powers, when harnessed, became heightened, accentuated, amplified.

Physicist Mae-Wan Ho informs us that "an organism arises when the loop of circulating energy somehow closes on itself to give a regenerating, reproducing, life cycle within which energy is mobilized, remaining stored as it is mobilized."[19] The circular form serves as the loop for the *closing off* of energy required in order for processes or organisms to arise; the circle allowing for necessary *circulation.*

In the creation of the cell by the early Earth, we find another example of the requirement for contained space. The

63

cell could not be created until it had a membrane, a system whereby the cell could close itself off to external influence. The membrane acts as a filter, screening carefully and intelligently what it allows in while preserving the integrity of the Center. Until a cell had a distinct boundary between outside and inside, it could not become an integral whole. Its energies were constantly dispersed into the environment that surrounded it.[20] The invention of the membrane out of fatty liposomes found in the early sea allowed the cell to maintain itself while interacting with the outside world. Similarly, the Earth's atmosphere offers a protective shield or boundary to the planet, allowing it to bring forth a wide variety of life forms, while acting as a screening device for UV radiation and other harmful cosmic substances. Without the protective circular embrace of the atmosphere, the planet would not be able to sustain life.

The stone circles created the same such boundary between ritual space and the everyday. Within the circular form, potent energies could be captured and enhanced at certain times. The circle provided the community or tribe with a solid center safe from external influences. We find the rounded form again in the kivas of the American Southwest, and the rounded Neolithic temples of Malta and Gozo.

Greene tells us of water's incredible ability to capture and contain cosmic moments by opening itself to a local impression, then closing itself around and holding the impression within until opened again. As in ritual space and the cell membrane, here we find again the idea of opening to a moment and then containing it within. Meditation, prayer, trance, and creative artistic endeavor can be seen as captured moments; impressions gathered in the container of intentionally created space.

The opening of water can happen by simply shaking it. It is

advised that water should be shaken before it is imbibed. Here we see water displaying the capacity toward memory. The trouble with water is that it lacks the ability to choose what it allows itself to be exposed to. It is open and accepting of everything, taking impressions from whatever it comes into contact with. This in itself could be an argument as to why water should be guarded and protected.

It also offers the opportunity for meditation on our part to consider the way we live. What are we choosing to open and expose ourselves to? What impressions are these things leaving on our being? How can we retain the integrity of our centers?

O = containment

The desire to flow or meander, combined with the striving for the spherical, can only lead to one outcome — the spiral. The meander, caught up within the dynamic form of held spherical space, begins to spin. Captured and spinning within this contained space, the powers and energies of flow become intensified, concentrated so that great creations and transformations can occur. The spiral is the primary creative form of the Universe, continually generating, regenerating, and bringing forth new evolutionary processes. We find the spiral form in the shell, the bark of trees, in the unfolding of plants, and in air patterns.

Even the heart, rather than being merely a pump, is a spiral circulating our blood and bodily fluids in a rhythmical, sustaining pattern. In the galactic realm, it is the great spiral galaxies that are creative, still actively engaged in birthing stars and planets.

The "atom itself seems more and more like the vortex or whirlpool ... continually self-creating by taking in and spitting out matter/energy while holding its form."[21]

Gimbutas interprets the spiral as the *Goddess's energy* and asserts that the placement of the spiral is important not for decoration, but as an "enhancement of that energy."[22] We find spirals spreading, swirling, coiling, and uncoiling over the breasts of the Goddess, and along her womb or buttocks. "The energy inherent in the continually moving forms awakens dormant life power and moves it forward."[23]

On Malta, the spiral image sprouts into plants, transformed into something physical, concrete. The Goddess's spiral energy is depicted as necessary — vital for anything's growth. "The spiraling force affects the germination and growth of trees and plants."[24]

In samples of water from a stream in Germany, Greene noticed that the macro invertebrates found in different parts in the stream reflected the formative activity she had detected in her drop pictures. In the part of the stream where the water was more pure, where it was able to form and hold vortices, she found more highly differentiated life forms.

All around us life processes uncoil, unfold, and unfurl as they blossom into being, becoming, as they make their journey toward the realization of potential locked deep within, a fern, fetuses, leaves, waves, larvae, seeds, and children. A human life also uncoils, unfurls — the journey taken is spiralform indeed. Gimbutas interprets the spiral as the spinning energy of the cosmos, as *cosmic evolution,* which transforms that which has encountered its "whooshing force." "Whirling signs seem to ensure a smooth transition from one phase to the next, from one cardinal direction to another."[25]

In the Chaco Canyon in present-day New Mexico in the American Southwest, circa 900-1295 BCE, lived what have come to be called the Anasazi people. Here again is evidence of a society that supersedes our expectations of knowledge or quality of life in early people. In Chaco Canyon are the remains of a large complex of buildings skillfully built into the canyon, complete with underground kivas and above-ground ritual areas. Many of the buildings are multistoried. A sophisticated irrigation system was discovered, as well as an enormous amount of pottery. The Anasazi found wealth in turquoise, which they mined and processed. The civilization thrived there for nearly 1,000 years. Though the complex was large enough to support 3,000 inhabitants, no more than 1,000 lived there at a time. This has led many to interpret it as a ritual center traveled to at certain times. Surrounding the complex is an intricate system of wide and clearly defined roads. The roads raise a large question for the simple reason that the Chacoans possessed not the wheel or the horse.

The Fatje Butte is a cliff face in the Chaco Canyon incised with two spirals upon which precise daggers of light fall at certain moments of importance throughout the seasonal year, including solstice, equinox, and particular lunar cycles.[26] Three deliberately cut and precisely aligned rock slabs that create patterns of light at specific and very precise times accomplish this phenomenon. The clocking of the exact moments of equinoxes and solstices is an achievement remarkable enough, but what intrigues me is that they chose the spiral form as the symbol onto which their carefully captured and focused sunlight should land. They could have chosen any shape, depiction, image. Petroglyphs abound in this canyon, yet they chose the spiral.

Chaco Canyon is not unique in focusing an intense form of the solstice sun onto the image of a spiral. At the passage tomb in Newgrange in County Meath, Ireland, the light of the midwinter solstice is captured through a rectangular opening above the linteled entryway to a tunnel that leads to an inner chamber. At the exact moment of midwinter solstice, the inner chamber of the tomb is illuminated by this deliberately captured light, revealing elegantly incised depictions of the spiral and the triple spiral that utterly fill this chamber. "Such symbols are necessary at critical moments ... when life powers are at stake."[27]

Early people believed that they must participate at these times, at equinox and solstice when the veil between the worlds is thin, when *the life powers are at stake.* One way to request for the continuation of these life powers would be to place a spiral, the symbol of the numinous generative life force of the Universe, at locations determined to be sacred. The intensely focused light of these cosmic power moments landing on the spiral may have been seen as an energizing of this force, promoting its renewal throughout the coming year or season.

Many native people, when asked about the petroglyphs, have stated that it is the Shamans who create them while in trance, or people who have been on a vision quest. Some say the spirit people have created them.

So too the San people of South Africa have said of their rock art that these are symbols from the spirit realm, depictions "of the world behind this one we see with our eyes"[28]

Researchers have compiled a list of images or *form constants* that are repeatedly encountered by people who have ingested hallucinogens or dropped into a trance state. The symbols recur worldwide and include the meander, the concentric circle, and the spiral.

Science has determined that certain forms or patterns exist and recur over and over. These forms are archetypal, generative forms that *give rise* to the physical world around us. These images possess and communicate a superconscious language, which early people interacted with in ritual. Placing these symbols at locations perceived to be where the *two worlds meet* would have been an act of great power.

Could we think of the Universe as a vast river meandering,

creating itself as it goes along? Its meandering setting things spinning, whirling into being, like water being changed by all that it encounters, changing all that is encountered by it? Could we think of the Universe as a body of water which, though it spreads itself across great distances, is still one single organism? As with the river flowing downstream—in which each piece of gravel and silt collected on its way through time has a part to play, as well as a say in the direction of that body of water—so too the presence of each atom, each element, and every organism plays a role in creating and sustaining the Universe. The sphere, the meander, and the spiral creative forms in this generative process.

It could be argued that these are simply metaphors, symbols used to convey an idea, a thought. True indeed. We must not forget, however, that language itself is a metaphor; words but symbols devised to describe the world around us. I have yet to encounter a word (in English) that conveys the range of depth and meaning expressed by the spiral. What one word would we use to say, "the sacred generative force at work in the Universe, available to us at every moment, present in every fraction of space"? I cannot think of one.

For now I will call it

Chapter Seven

Mountains

Working with Mountains, Step 1: Your Local Mountains

I t is essential for a medicine person to know her local mountains. They are the foundation for any medicine work. Mountains are large entities that house within them many smaller entities. They must be approached with the greatest caution and respect. Mountains offer orientation, strength, support, and sustenance to humans, animals, and elemental beings. Once you have created the proper relationship with them, they offer this to your medicine work as well.

Everyone has a home mountain they were born under that holds their family history. In the West African Dagara cosmology, the mountains hold all of our ancestral stories and memories. The local mountains where you now live function this way as well, holding the memories of the land all the way back to their formation inside the stars. In this tradition, there are five elements: fire, water, mineral, Earth, and the wild. Mountains are part of the element of mineral. Minerals are the rocks and bones and stones of the Earth. Any rock or stone is a fractal of the larger mountain, and can be used to make offerings to the element of mineral to them.

In the Italian tradition, the living relationship with the

mountains is essential. One must learn how to "eat the mountain." To the Streghe, the mountains are the wombs of the Earth. The womb is a mountain of ancestral memory and wisdom within the female body. Taking care of the mountains takes care of women's wombs as well. We must listen to the mountains and the wise wombs of women in order to live our lives in balance with the Earth. Being intimate with the mountains is one way to do this.

To form a relationship with your local mountains, first you need to know who they are. Who is the tall peak on your landscape and horizon that you see every day, or see most fully when you journey about in your car? What is her current name? Do you know her earlier name? Typically, if you ask, the mountain will tell you the name by which she calls herself.

After you locate her, begin to interact with her from afar. Call to her. "Eat her." Make offerings to her from where you live. Pour water onto a rock in your yard or at your local park, telling her you wish for the way to be clear for you to form a relationship with her. Listen for a response. Take time to do this until you feel called to her.

This is your beginning first step.

Working with Mountains, Step 2: Going to the Mountain

After you have spent some time communing with the mountain from afar, you may begin to plan your journey to her. The first journey, or even first few, have no agenda. You are going to meet the mountain, walk upon her, and get to know her. Be aware of the intention in your heart. Bring her gifts just as you would when you visit anyone who has welcomed you to her home. Offer for the sake of offering, not to receive something in return.

Becoming intimate with your chosen mountain takes time.

Be very patient. It is something that grows organically from a relationship that is cultivated slowly. It is something that is bestowed to you by the mountain. You will know when this happens. No other but the mountain can bestow this medicine to you. Others can guide and mentor you, but the mountain is the bestower.

Before you go, tell the mountain that you are coming. Even now, after being in relationship with a local mountain for many years, I still ask before I go if the way is clear for me to come. I ask if there are special offerings needed from me on the day I plan to go. There will be times when the mountain says, "No, do not come today." Respect this and trust that she has her reasons.

Before you go to the mountain, ask for protection from your personal guides, be they animal totem, gods and goddesses, Mother Mary, or ancestors. Bring them with you as you go. They will lead the way in this new relationship. They will direct you to the places and pathways on the mountain that are resonant with you.

The first few trips are journeys of discovery. Simply go and feel the place. The most important quality to bring is that of deep listening. Remain open in heart and mind to what is being said there, both physically and spiritually.

Working with Mountains, Step 3: The Guardian and the Wild Beings

Once you have visited the mountain a few times, you may notice a guardian near the beginning of your chosen pathway. Often this is a tree, a large rock, or outcropping. This guardian being is a gatekeeper for the other entities who reside on the mountain. The guardian is the first being to be acknowledged in your visits from now forward. Greet the guardian by making offerings of your choice. By working with the guardian, the mountain entities will reveal themselves to you.

The mountain will only open itself to you a bit at a time. If approached correctly, this is how you build trust and open the door to further teachings. That is why the guardian is greeted each time you go, because we are never done learning. Think of the guardian as the cosmic bouncer, guarding the door to all that lies beyond. I always stop for some time at the guardian to listen for guidance on my trip that day.

Some may perceive the guardian to be a being inside the tree or rock. It may appear as an animal, a personified god or goddess, an angel, or all of the above. You may also perceive different beings at different times. Rather than seeing something, some may hear something, others will sense something. All ways of perceiving are fine. What is important is their message.

Near the guardian, at the beginning of each hike on the mountain, I also make an offering to the wild animals that live on the mountain. The wild animals keep the mountain ecosystem alive and well functioning. Though we rarely see them, they are the keepers of the mountain and must be acknowledged for that. It is they who allow us to be there in safety. When you honor the wild, remember the top predators, even if they are no longer there—the wolves, for example, who are still there in spirit form. It is important for you to acknowledge them, as well as the wedeme and kontomble of the place.

For my offering to the wild, I often leave dog cookies or cat food, water, red liquid to represent a blood offering, spirits (alcohol) of any sort, and some of the snacks I bring for myself that day. As I make my offering, I thank the wild beings for remaining wild and recognize their essential presence. I ask them to keep me safe on my journey and offer appreciation to them for all the times they have protected me and allowed me to be there.

Honoring the guardian beings and the wild are the key to your next step, which is slowly meeting who lives on the mountain.

For more instruction on how to work with entities and beings on mountains, see my book: *Teachings From the Trees: Spiritual Mentoring from the Standing Ones.*

Chapter Eight

Elemental Forces

The Queen of the Underworld and Her Sister: Cosmic Justice

When one is initiated as a stick diviner in the Dagara tradition, she is given a kit with "pieces" (objects such as stones, small branches, and shells) in it to use when she divines. These *pieces* not only represent, but are in fact living entities and energies. A particular stone is Earth, another mountain; an abalone shell is water. Certain *pieces* are selected by the diviner's stick for the divination at hand. These are the beings that are speaking to the person who is receiving the divination that day.

One of the pieces in the kit is a small branch from a tree that has been struck by lightning. Powerful and mysterious, it holds a separate entity on either end. One end of this piece is "Cosmic Justice," the other is described as "health." The diviner must determine which entity is coming through on that piece each time it is selected. I won't use their Dagara names here because it is considered a bad idea to say these entities' names aloud. These entities exist by different names in almost every tradition. They are far from unique to the Dagara. In the West, we know them as the *Queen of the Underworld*, and her sister, *Cosmic Justice*.

How is it that these two seemingly unrelated beings inhabit the same piece in the divination kit? This is a good subject to explore.

Cosmic Justice

When I first began to do divinations, when this *piece* presented itself as *Cosmic Justice*, a being I perceived as an archangel appeared in the room. Before I began divining, I was not even sure I believed in archangels. I had heard about a hierarchy of angelic beings, but I did not know it as a truth or a reality. I also did not understand it. But here I was, doing a divination with an archangel in the room as I held *Cosmic Justice* in my hand. In fact, these beings do exist and they are a commanding presence.

How do I know they are archangels? Because archangels are the ones who wield a sword. This is the sword that cuts through, the sword that maintains balance. This sword is not for battling in the way we commonly think of it. This is the sword of justice. This is the sword of precision. This is the sword of Truth.

When the beings of *Cosmic Justice* come into a divination, they are always there to "right a wrong" for the person who has come for divination. This "wrong that needs righting" can take on many different forms, but it is clear that somewhere, something has gone terribly wrong. A "violation" has occurred. This violation can be karmic, an event in their ancestral line, or a circumstance in their present lifetime. Whatever the violation is, it needs attending to in order for this person to go on and have a satisfying life, and for their descendents to do the same. Attending to this will also heal the past.

The keepers of *Cosmic Justice* are the ones who must

maintain balance on the cosmic scale. It is not for humans to understand this, because we actually cannot. Our perspective is too small. But it *is* for humans to listen to when they show up, and it *is* for humans to live within these cosmic laws, otherwise it creates an energetic imbalance.

The keepers of *Cosmic Justice* are also known as elemental forces of great strength and power that humans have absolutely no control over. They are lightning and earthquakes; they are fierce winds we call hurricanes, they are tornadoes, they are thunder. This is the magnitude of their power. They are often dark-feathered beings and can show up as the one called *Thunderbird*. Egyptian *Ma'at*, with her Feather of Truth and Scales of Justice, fits this category as well. Indeed, they all take many forms. I can be sure I am in the presence of one of them by the depth of humility evoked in me, the diviner.

The Queen of the Underworld and "Health"

When we see and experience manifestations of what we call illness—lack of health in our bodies, families, our systems, our governments, and ecosystems, and indeed in our own mental states—when we experience *dis-ease.* This is where the scales have tipped so far into imbalance that the "lightning piece" comes to speak of its other end: issues around "health." Now we are in the realm of the sister of *Cosmic Justice,* the *Queen of the Underworld.*

Though it is true in the larger context, it is not enough to say *we cause our own illness.* Illness is a more complex picture than the small one humans hold. Lack of health is a symptom; a sign that something is out of balance. When an imbalance manifests into a physical form, it means this has gone on for some time, and is no longer held only in the energetic realms. Now it is physical. Epidemics may be looked at this way, but there is no direct cause and effect. Beware of those simplistic assumptions. The person afflicted may not be directly related to the offense, but their symptom can be informative to us, and their healing can help on many levels. If we truly know how to listen, we may actually understand. In fact, traditionally when this piece shows up as "health" in a divination, it could be a health issue for anyone in the person's family. It is letting us know there is an imbalance in the *system*.

When these kinds of symptoms show up, and when this end of the piece comes forward in a divination, it is time to do more than go to the doctor. We need to pay a visit to the *Queen of the Underworld*, journey into the depths of our own or the collective darkness, to face our shadows, and release our cherished yet limiting beliefs.

The sister of *Cosmic Justice*, the *Queen of the Underworld*, is also known as Sumerian Inanna's sister, *Ereshkigal*; Greek Demeter's daughter, *Persephone/Kore*; Norse *Hel*; Egyptian *Nepthys*; and the *Black Virgins*. These are but some of the names for the Goddess that lives deep inside the inner Earth. These dark underworld Goddesses are the ones we must take the labyrinthine path toward when health is at risk, at the personal, family, or community level.

Researcher Eva Meyerowitz writes that in the Akan tradition from West Africa, the Supreme Goddess *Nyame* split herself into three parts, one of which is *the underworld personification of Nyame*. One of the names of this Underworld Goddess in the Akan tradition is *Aberewa*. This name is stunningly close to the name for this entity in the Dagara tradition. Meyerowitz also reports that *Aberewa* is related to the planet Jupiter, and represented by a rod of iron and meteorites.[29] We know from a scientific point of view that the core of this planet, Earth, is made of molten iron. When I found this information about the Underworld Goddess in the

Akan tradition, connections between these two entities residing on this same piece from a lightning tree fell into place.

I was excited to find these two entities connected again in the Greek Tradition in Peter Kingsley's *In the Wisdom of Dark Places*. Kingsley writes that the Goddess of *Cosmic Justice* holds open the gates to this underworld realm for all who need to make the journey. They work together, these two, *Cosmic Justice* and the *Queen of the Underworld*, interacting to maintain balance.[30]

In Ancient Greece, humans retreated to underground temples at times of illness for healing. Knowing that they had been taken into a state of imbalance by something larger than themselves, they wished to commune with the Underworld Goddess to heal themselves. They made the literal journey to her through one of her temples for dream incubation and the deep listening that can only be arrived at through stillness.

This tradition of dream incubation and *Descent to the Goddess* did not begin with the Ancient Greeks. This is a tradition found in Sumeria in the myth of the Goddess Inanna, and before that back to the Neolithic Goddess cultures as well. The underground temples of Malta, which predate Ancient Greece by thousands of years, had such dream incubation temples with the Dreaming Goddess at their core. These kinds of temples are found all across the planet in Neolithic and Bronze Age cultures. Before that, humans retreated to painted caves. This is an ancient human tradition—one the Greek philosophers learned from the *priestess-diviners* before them.

There is one sure way to meet these two entities, and that is through physical death, but the ancients knew, and indigenous cultures still do, that it is important to practice dying while we are living, or *"die before we die,"* as Kingsley puts it.

What we need to learn to do most of all right now is listen to both of these entities—feel how they are indeed two parts of one whole.

If we can allow ourselves to listen to the *Queen of the Underworld* and her sister *Cosmic Justice* once again, we will find a way to restore balance and bring healing.

All of this is yet another reason to bring divination and ritual back to the forefront of our culture.

Chapter Nine

Siura: Soul and Source Soul

Keeping Clean All the Varying Levels of That Which We Call "Soul"

I n the ancient Akan tradition, the *kra* (soul) is the *flash of fire* from the Supreme Goddess Nyame that sparks us into life. Without the spark of Nyame, we are not alive. Nyame gives us life. She enlivens matter. We carry a piece of her inside us; the Great Mother, the Original Source. This is our soul.

In *The Sacred State of the Akan*, Eva Meyerowitz writes about the *Akra-Dware* ritual. The *Akra-Dware* is a ritual purification of the soul. In this ceremony, the *soul bearers* for the king perform this ritual on his behalf. The *soul bearers* wear white, as white symbolizes purity and peace. They paint white forms and symbols on their bodies with chalk and wear the *kra disc* on a cord from plant fibers around their necks.[31]

The ritual is a cleansing of the soul in the river. The soul bearers carry the soul, or *kra*, to the river in a *kra basin*. Often this is a gold basin. The king's soul, or *kra*, is kept clean and purified for the good of all his people. They pray for the purity and vitality of the king's *kra* because the condition of his soul affects them all. They make prayers and offerings to his *kra*.

They feed it.

In this ritual, the soul of the king is washed for the good of the whole community. Before kingship, the Akan culture was a matriarchy with Queenmothers. At that time, this was a washing of the soul of the Queenmother. In Pharaonic Egypt, there was a strong belief that the pharaoh held the soul for all of his community members. He was responsible for keeping his soul clean and in right alignment with the gods and goddesses for the good of his people.

Though most of us no longer live in monarchies, this concept of keeping one soul clean for the good of all souls still holds true. There are varying degrees and levels of soul. What one does to purify and cleanse any level of soul, one does for the good of all souls, including the individual soul, group soul, Earth soul, and cosmic soul.

What do I mean by this? Most cultures hold the concept of an energetic component that exists beyond our physical bodies and incarnations, and connects us to the larger *Source*. In Egypt, it is the *ka;* in Akan, the *kra;* in Dagara, it is the *sie*. There are many more we can add to this list from traditions all over the planet. In English, we tend to call this "soul." We all have a personal soul, a group soul, and an ancestral soul, which may or may not be one and the same. And we are all also part of the larger cosmic soul: the Source soul.

All of these components are part of one whole, sometimes called the *world soul*. Anything we do to benefit one level of the soul benefits the whole.

The Individual Soul and the *Siura*

In the Dagara tradition, there is the *sie*, the individual soul of the person. This is not the same as the physical part or "skin" of the person. There is also the *siura*, that which connects the individual soul to the Source or Cosmic Soul. The *siura*—that which connects us to Source—is an alive entity. *Siura* is sometimes translated as the *guardian spirit* of our soul. This translation makes sense in that keeping us connected to Source guards our soul from harm. The *siura* is the umbilicus to the nurturing sustenance of the Goddess—the Original Source; the Source soul. We cannot live without this connection. When this connection is strong and robust, we feel supported, loved, and have a strong sense of belonging.

The *siura* is also a piece[32] in the diviner's kit. Issues that come through when this piece is chosen in a divination can indicate soul loss or damage, and risk of spiritual and physical death.

When this piece is selected by the stick in divination, I am often given a picture of the child-self (*inner child*) of the person who is receiving the divination. This indicates to me where in the trajectory of this person's life some degree of "soul loss" or "disconnection" occurred. The "child" being often wishes to be reconnected or "found." Rituals and offerings are prescribed to carry this out. In our North American culture, much soul loss seems to happen in childhood. In other cultures, this is not the case. We don't really "lose" our soul; our connection to Source becomes frayed and we become fragmented. Restoration of wholeness is needed.

The Group Soul

Until a few years ago, the concept of *group soul* made sense to me intellectually, but I had not yet experienced it. The experience I had of the group soul is one of the single most epiphanic moments of my life. I will attempt to convey it here.

During a visit home to New Hampshire, some family members and I decided to go to the cemetery and pay respect to our ancestors. My father and brothers had been to the ancestral land in Italy, and wished to spread some of the soil from there on the graves of the ancestors here. We are a very large, Italian-American family, and many of our ancestors are buried in the same Catholic cemetery. My great-grandmother, the Strega, is buried there as well.

After we performed the ritual of the soil, I knelt down over her grave to offer her some special attention. I had my spirit bell with me, as well as vodka, water, and ash. With my fingers, I lovingly cleaned away the grass and dirt overgrowing her name marker and brushed the soil and debris from the engraved letters. I surrounded the marker with ash. As I was about to pour the water and vodka onto it as blessing and offering, my niece, who was 10 at the time, came up and asked, "May I ring your bell while you do that?"

Surprised by the perceptiveness of this offer, I replied, "It would be my honor."

She picked up the iron spirit bell and began to ring it.

I poured the vodka and water onto the granite marker. As I did so, I was overcome with a strange sensation. I saw my great-grandmother in spirit form above me, as well as an image of her body buried in the Earth below me. Concurrently, I saw myself in bird's-eye view pouring the vodka and water over her gravestone, and my niece beside me ringing the bell. I experienced these pictures in geometric formations that interlocked and intersected each other. These multidimensional images showed me that in some very magical way, we were all the same being. This is not to say that we were the same *person;* it was not that at all, since we were clearly individuated, two of us currently embodied as separate people. Rather, this *vision* was showing me that we are, though in separate bodies, components of one whole story — a group soul. There may be more who are part of this group. I am sure it is not just we three.

I understood in that moment that how I show up or do not show up to my life affects both of theirs. I not only affect my own life with the choices I make in my trajectory, but also all of those in my "pod." Any action I take, or fail to take, in my life tugs at their trajectories, even the great-grandmother who is dead. Though "dead," souls are still on a trajectory. In fact, in this moment I understood how one can be an ancestor and an embodied human at the same time. The "soul" is a multivalent being, with many articulations at once.

This was a wake-up call for me. I was grateful to my great-grandmother, who had shown up to her life in a brave and valiant way. I was sure it contributed to the parts I like best about myself. I also committed to try, to the best of my ability, to show up to my life with integrity and ferocity of focus for the young one standing beside me, that she may have an easier ride through hers.

The Cosmic or *Source* Soul

It is not enough to know or believe that we have a soul or group soul. We must know that our soul is connected to and nourished by the larger soul of the cosmos, and that our soul also feeds this larger soul.

We all came from Original Fire. We are sparks, forever connected. We are both creator and created, individual soul and cosmic soul at once. Understanding connection to Source, being thankful for it and praising it, is essential. By believing in Source, we give ourselves the gift of believing in ourselves.

Though our souls are a part, they also contain the whole. Our souls are a fractal of the whole, of Source, the whole cosmos. Yes, we really are that.

Source or Goddess is continually sustaining and creating

the cosmos. You may have another way of conceptualizing this presence. You may call it the One, you may call it God. For me, since all comes from the Mother—the one who continues to birth us every minute of every day; our Source—it is naturally female. Goddess. She, with her luminous light, continues to nourish and feed us as long as the connection is strong.

Soul Arises Organically from Collective Experience

A soul arises organically from the collected experience of a being. Souls evolve and change through time, retaining "signatures" and something akin to that which we call memory. There are many kinds of souls. Anything that is alive is ensouled. As humans, we have free will and we also have choice. Within the context of the gift of free will, the choices we make determine the outcome of our experiences. These choices create the palette of the soul that we continue to create from through multiple lifetimes. The soul is a field made up of these gathered experiences. Just as our individual souls arise organically from our individual experiences, the group soul also arises from the collective experience of the beings in the group. This soul continues to evolve and grow through time as well.

The soul of the cosmos (soul of the Goddess) arises organically from the collective experience of Source, which includes all of us, individual and group.

Soul Cleaning

In divination, there are many ways the need for a cleansing of the soul can show up. Soul washings, sweeps, and removal of toxic "dirt" are also often prescribed.

Keeping ourselves clean and pure keeps the cosmos clean

and pure. The cosmos is a fractal reality. Any toxic "dirt" we clean in ourselves helps to clean up the "dirt" in the larger source soul. Group soul washings can serve the purpose of cleansing the soul of a community and more.

The cleansing is not to imply guilt or create shame; rather, it is to simply keep it all clean. After all, we love our Mother — the Goddess, Source — and we want to help keep Her clean by keeping ourselves clean. This is similar to not wanting to pollute or soil something we love. Having this respect for the cosmic soul, and understanding that we are part of that, creates respect for ourselves and all of life. It is a deep honoring of the sacred inner mystery of the universe that we each carry within ourselves.

Chapter Ten

Entities of the "Space Above"

Saazumwin: The Light Bringers

The *Saazumwin* are pure light—star beings. They are the *Light Bringers*. In Dagara cosmology, the *Saazumwin* are entities of *saazu*, the "space above."[33] They are "the ones who stretch between the stars and the Earth."[34]

They are group minded, but can also individuate. They hold Galactic Consciousness. The *Saazumwin* are beneficent. They are portals to the stars. They have a deep connection to water.

I often experience the *Saazumwin* as light tunnels. Other times they appear as angels, or large white birds. I often see *Saazumwin* around a person who has come for divination.

There is a lot of "light" in the universe that we cannot see. Different parts of the light spectrum are visible and nonvisible to the human eye. The *Saazumwin* are alive in the full spectrum. To eliminate further confusion, I will use the broad word "light" to mean this full spectrum. (For a further elucidation of the light spectrum, see my article "Electromagnetism: A Circuitous, Nonlinear Affair" in Appendix B of this book).

Star Beings and *Saazumwin*

We are each connected to a star — our star of origin. When the *Saazumwin* piece is chosen by the stick in divination[35] it can indicate that a person's "star needs polishing."[36] This may refer to agreements that were made before birth, and the need to remember our starry origin.

In many divinations, I am shown a link between women's ovaries and stars. I do not fully understand what this means yet, but when this happens the follicles — cells that will become fertile eggs on the woman's ovaries — light up as, simultaneously, a star lights up in the sky. This may mean the potentiality exists for an individuated intelligence that lives in the star to be transferred to the woman's ovary, and if she so chooses, birthed through her body. The potentiality in the star has the feeling of what we call *consciousness*. It is not yet a human. Allowing or disallowing this potentiality to come to fruition is up to the individual woman. But there is the potentiality, and what even feels like the request, by this consciousness located in the star.

Other times when I am shown these kinds of configurations between ovaries and stars in a divination, a star association is being revealed to the person receiving the divination through the mother line. This image showing up in a divination may be revealing purpose or a healing that is needed. No matter what it means, there is a clear correlation between ovaries and stars.

Women carry these connections and potentialities within their bodies. Mothers carry these bonds for their sons. The mother line holds this part of our connectedness to the greater cosmos. Children really do come from or through the stars.

This is a vast spectrum to explore; however, it is clear that the mechanism for human incarnation is mediated through this linking between the stars and the ovaries. Ovaries are the eggs that produce eggs and cycle with the moon. The whole endocrine system is in touch with these greater forces. This cosmic connection allows a woman to create life from within herself.

The *Saazumwin* oversee and guard this star connection. They often have a grandmotherly feel when they come in this capacity. But there are also personal *Saazumwin* who feel childlike and elfin: *star elementals.*

Precious Light

There is precious little light in the universe. Only four percent of the universe is what scientists refer to as *luminous matter* – matter that is detectable by our current scientific instruments of detection. Ninety-six percent of the universe is *other* – classified as "dark." The interplay of light and dark is a mystery, but that relationship illuminates reality in every moment. Earth is a vast, mysterious darkness that agreed to be enlivened by the light.[37] Earth is in intimate connection with the *Saazumwin*. As the inner darkness of our bodies is regulated by the light through our endocrine glands, so too the Earth system is regulated through interactions with the light. (For more on this subject, see Appendix B in this book)

If we believe the Earth is an alive and intelligent entity – Gaia – so too must be the stars. The stars have a physical body, but also other dimensional forms; what we might call a spiritual existence. The *Saazumwin* are the spiritual, unseen dimension of a star: *the spiritual dimension of light.*

Delivering the Light

The inner Earth is dark. We, with our human bodies and hearts, can participate in intentionally receiving the light from the *Saazumwin* and delivering it to the inner Earth.

When we do this, the beings that inhabit the inner Earth — Earth elementals — receive this as a gift of heat and warmth. It feeds them. Many group rituals with stones can do this as well. This seems to be what was happening at a lot of the stone circles in Neolithic times.

The Trees Can Teach Us How

There are light patterns that we each come in with. Some of them match up and resonate. We carry these with us from the stars. The trees hold these patterns in their bodies. We can reconnect with the patterns of the stars by listening to the trees. The trees are holding this wisdom for us. There is a deep relationship between the *Saazumwin* and the trees that also wants to be remembered at this time on the planet. These connections all want to be reestablished. Collaboration among all is being asked for once again. The biggest gift we can offer right now to the trees, the Earth, the elemental beings, and the *Saazumwin* is our listening.

The Stars, the *Saazumwin*, and the Water

The *Saazumwin* are deeply connected to the water. This connection would like to be strengthened now on Earth. There are two simple rituals you can engage in to help with this, *to return the stars to the water.*

At the dark time of the moon, go to the water. Ask the water which flower it would like to receive for this cycle. Once you receive the information, collect the flower and offer it to the water. If you cannot acquire the flower locally, you may show the water a picture of the flower or offer the essence of the flower through tincture or flower essence. *This ritual offers attunement between the water and the stars.*

At the time of the full moon, go and ask which mineral the water needs. Once you determine it, offer it to the water. The minerals are the connection between the stars and the inner Earth. *This ritual allows the stars to reach the deep.*

The stars created all the elements in their bodies. Earth is a further articulation of this creative process. Consciously engaging the *Saazumwin* brings more interactive participation to this process. Begin with gentleness and no preconceptions, and see what is revealed to you.

The Star Grandmothers

The Star Grandmothers first came to me through a sacred place in Sonoma County, California, now called the *Laguna de Santa Rosa*. This holy ground once housed three deep lakes called the "Diamond Lakes" by the First People/Pomo and Miwok Indians who populate this region. This wetland area, which was under 20 to 30 feet of water every winter, was considered the heart and center of their world and community.[38]

Before the Mexicans and Europeans arrived, this was a place of great abundance. In the summer months, the Indians gathered in temporary villages around the Laguna. Summer gatherings were held here with ritual and celebration of this bounty.

In the unfortunate way most of these stories turn out, the Laguna also suffered great trauma at the incursion and arrival of the Mexicans and Europeans, who dynamited these Diamond Lakes in order to fill them in for farmland and diverge the pathway of the water for their new city of Santa Rosa. It is almost impossible to try to understand the worldview that could look at such beauty, and decide that it

92

needed to be bombed and drained. But that is indeed what came to pass.

What is left now is a faint echo of this place. There is still a wetland lagoon (the Laguna) that collects overflow water from the Russian River in the winter. Efforts are in place to restore and preserve what remains of this precious place, but the Diamond Lakes are no longer here in physical form, and most people don't know they ever were.

When we hear about these kinds of trauma to the Earth, we often focus on the physical losses to the ecosystem, including animals and embodied humans, but what about the spiritual/energetic component? What happens to the spirits and the ancestors of the land, both human and other, when places experience such violation? What about the spirits of the trees and the rocks? What about the elemental beings of a place? What happens to them in times of crisis and trauma? Surely there is a deeper, spiritual layer that must be considered in our current efforts to heal and restore natural landscapes and make proper compensation to a place and people wounded and displaced by previous devastating actions. Many of us of various ancestries who now live on this land are called to participate in this healing.

The Sebastopol Community Cultural Center now stands on part of the Laguna de Santa Rosa. I went there to teach a course, *Writing as Spiritual Practice*, a couple of years ago in which I led a shamanic journey with a drum. In our journeying, our small group immediately met energetic beings, both ancestors of the land and local entities, still residing at the Laguna. They had stories to tell us.

The Star Grandmothers were among the first to show up for me. I had never heard the phrase "the Star Grandmothers" before I met these beings. They told me they were there; that they had been there long before what we think of as the First

People of this land. They seemed to be their ancestors. Long before what current historical records tell us, they were here — very early people — and they were very much involved in interacting with and holding star energy in this place of the Diamond Lakes. They showed me many of the rituals they carried out, one of which was them sitting around the water and toning to the stars. They said they were pulling the stars down into the water, making what they were calling "star soup" in the lake.

They showed me initiations they carried out there with the young women and men, merging them with their *Kachinas*. They used the word *Kachina*, which surprised me as that seemed to be a term local to mostly the Hopi and associated tribes of the Southwest. I acknowledge my ignorance here and apologize for any glaring errors. I am not indigenous to this place. My ancestors are from Europe. However, I have come to understand that entities in the other dimensions speak to us in ways we can understand using the material of our own psyche to do so. Using the word *Kachinas*, one I had heard and had a vague understanding of, was a way for them to help me understand what they were trying to convey. Surely there was a different word used locally for the similar entities here, but the Star Grandmothers were using this term since it held a similar vibration and configuration in my psyche to what they were trying to communicate.

I wanted to listen to what was trying to come through. It seemed they were showing me a deep connection between the humans, the stars, the elemental forces, and the elemental beings of this place. It seemed the elemental forces and elemental beings were in this category of what they were calling the *Kachinas*.

The way this was being presented to me was resonant with the Dagara teachings and cosmology I am initiated into.

94

Perhaps I was being shown how these relationships manifest/constellate here in North America. Perhaps they were resonant with the ways the Dagara hold their relationships to the kontomble/wedeme (elemental beings) and the elemental forces, and there was something for me to understand in this resonance. I believe now they are, and that this was indeed part of what they were trying to show me. Was there a relationship between the elemental beings and elemental forces similar to the Dagara configuration that was wanting to be remembered and reactivated here in this place?

I am not African or Native American. My personal spiritual lineage is Italian. I was born into a Strega lineage through my Italian-American ancestors who immigrated to New Hampshire, but I am continuously shown that all these lineages wish to work together in concert now to return to the Earth Her Medicine, the one taproot from which all spiritual lineages emerge. Being shown similarities between varying lineages helps to deepen our understanding of the diverse individual lines, and teaches us what is wanting to happen now at this Time on Gaia, and what our role as Earth workers can be.

Much wisdom was lost, fragmented, and went underground in times of colonization and persecution. Much of this wisdom now wants to return. Returning to proper relationship with the elemental forces and the elemental beings of a place is one of the most important parts of this reclaiming. Being shown how these relationships manifested in all the different cultures and lineages helps us begin to restore these essential relationships. If the Star Grandmothers were showing me that they had merged their young people with their *Kachinas* in group initiation ceremonies, similar to the Dagara initiations of merging with an elemental being (kontomble/wedeme) to become a diviner, then this must have

95

been an important part of their cosmology as well, and one they wanted remembered.

The Star Grandmothers told me there had come a time of persecution for them, a time where they were intentionally decimated. They were using this word *decimated* very purposefully. This was long, long ago, way before the arrival of the Mexicans or Europeans. I tried to see who carried this out, who came and destroyed them, but I could not, nor could I see a clear timeline of when these events had occurred.

The Star Grandmothers told me the later persecutions/ decimations of the First People/Indians that we know about could not have taken place unless this had happened first. The decimation of the Star Grandmothers and their wisdom had created the pathways for later genocides. They said those who came had deliberately set out to destroy the women and the women's medicine that was so strong in this place at the time of the Star Grandmothers. And that is what they did.

The Star Grandmothers saw this coming and went into the water. They said they became the frogs. Their wisdom is still here, only dormant and waiting in the water. They want us to bring it to the surface once again.

You too may listen to the Star Grandmothers and all that they want to tell us and return to us at this time. If that is your intention, you may make an offering of milk to your local waterway, telling the Star Grandmothers you are ready to listen to what they have to say. If your intention is pure, and your heart is clear, they will begin to speak to you.

Chapter Eleven

Moon Journal

What do we really know and understand about the moon? I fear very little. This chapter is dedicated to deepening our understanding of the moon and our relationship to it. The Rumi poem below captures the spirit with which I enter into this process of discovery.

Some Kiss We Want

There is some kiss we want
With our whole lives, the touch

of spirit on the body. Seawater
begs the pearl to break it shell.

And the lily, how passionately
it needs some wild darling!

At night I open the window and ask

the moon to come and press its

face against mine

breathe into me. Close

The language door and open the love-window.

The moon won't use the door,

only the window.

Rumi

(Translation by Coleman Barks)

The Moon, the Sun, the Earth and the Ovaries

Some people love shoes, handbags, American History, the occult, basketball, or soccer. It can be anything. These loves can become obsessions, and before we know it they have taken over a part of us and own us in some way.

Me? I am infatuated with images of double eggs uncovered in the pottery remains of the Neolithic Cucuteni Culture of Eastern Europe. These are images that haunt me. Obsessed, I spend time copying, drawing, redrawing, and coloring them. I look at them for long periods of time, asking what they have to tell me. To my mind they are alive and moving, speaking of life and life energy, creative power and process.

People who populated a culture near the Black Sea 6,000 years ago painted these eggs onto plates, bowls, and the outside of pots. The Cucuteni was a large and successful culture in what spans present-day Russia, Moldavia, Romania, and the Ukraine. One of the earliest pottery wheels was discovered in the remains of the Cucuteni, as well as some of the most outstanding artistic images of the Neolithic Era.

In their pottery workshops, the Cucuteni people also created female figures covered with swirling and twirling lines. Spirals run across their large hips. When broken open, many of them reveal two eggs nestled within the womb space. The person who put them there knew no one would see them unless they were broken open. They put them there nonetheless. Double eggs are a theme of this culture. (For more information on the Cucuteni Culture see "The Archetype of the Womb, Part II: Womb Ovens," located in Appendix A of this book.)

Neolithic Understanding of Cell Division?

The Cucuteni double-egg images that I adore are skillfully painted, twin ovals held within a circle or cell-like structure. Rows of waving snake lines run across and through the whole cell, connecting the eggs, unifying it all. In some, the dual eggs are defined and separate; in others, they open to each other, the snake lines running through the place where they connect. In one image there are dots held within the separated eggs, one above and one below the waving snakeline. In general, the Cucuteni painted black-on-red designs.

When I first saw these images, they spoke to me of dynamic movement, energy stimulation, energetic streams, and creation.[39] Then they began to look like cell division. At the time I told myself I was crazy. There was no way Neolithic people could have known about cell division.

Surely, ancient people had access to many eggs – bird eggs, amphibian eggs. Without doubt they also opened them up, explored them, observed their many phases of development...but access to human eggs? Mammalian eggs?

99

Human cells? To understand that those cells divide and sometimes become people?

The Cucuteni artists who created the female figures with eggs nestled inside them had some idea of where reproductive cells are located in a human female. Are these depictions of human ovaries—the eggs that make eggs within the human female body? The truth is, I will never know the intention of the designer of these Cucuteni eggs. They lived thousands of years ago and are inaccessible to me now, but I do know the journey these images have taken me on.

Moon Over Ovary

Each month (moon) the ovaries, upon prompting from the pituitary gland's follicle stimulating hormone (FSH), begin to prepare about 20 cells (germ cells), eventually ending up with one chosen ripe egg out of one chosen ripe follicle. The cell within the follicle that will become an egg is called an oocyte (oh-a-cite). Many of the words describing ovaries have double O's. They are derived from the Greek word for egg, ōion. Double O's, double eggs, double cells. Cell division, duplication, replication, reproduction, doubling.

Oophrectomy is to remove one or both ovaries; oogenesis is the production or development of an ovum; oophoritis is inflammation of the ovary, and so on. The full oocyte is released into the fallopian tube, but the follicle lives on, continuing its phases. Like the moon, every month of a fertile woman's life, a follicle waxes to fullness, and wanes to diminishment in an almost identical 28-day cycle. We, the female of the species, have a moon on our ovaries. The word *moon* also has two O's, a double O. The Cucuteni eggs are double O's, the moon within us.

Romancing the Oocyte

On a webpage detailing in visual images the process of mammalian oogenesis, I found startling similarities to my cherished Cucuteni egg designs. In the images of what are called the secondary follicle containing a secondary oocyte, my mind registered recognition. The secondary follicle is the follicle that has been chosen by the body to mature its oocyte through a series of steps in meiosis. The secondary oocyte in these images had just completed the second step in meiosis.

The Cucuteni images looked like double or mirror images of the secondary or mature oocyte within the secondary follicle. The secondary oocyte is the largest cell in the human body and is just visible to the human eye. It is possible Neolithic people actually did have a chance to see these cells.

The death ritual called "excarnation" was common in the Neolithic. This is a process where the bodies of the dead were left out in special places to allow the vultures to eat the flesh and clean the bones. After this, the bones were recovered and buried in special tombs or places to keep the ancestors and their memories near. Different stages of fertility and reproduction could have been observed in this process.

Also found in the archaeological remains of this culture were many ovens in the shape of wombs. Perhaps through these observations, the Cucuteni also developed an understanding of the womb as the alchemical "oven" that it is.[40]

There are two forms of cell division, mitosis and meiosis. These two forms of cell division are responsible for the presence of life on this planet. In this process, DNA gets copied and stored. The process of mitosis is a cell reproducing by making an identical copy of itself. This goes on everywhere—in our bodies, in plants, bacteria, and more. It is a process developed on Earth by early bacteria some four billion years ago.

The process of meiosis is different in that it is a sex cell that divides its chromosomes in half so that it can mix or share DNA with another cell during reproduction. These sex cells are also called "germ cells." Out of meiosis emerges an entirely new being, unlike mitosis, which is a replication of the same being. Meiosis arose on Earth about one billion years ago, and is called *sexual reproduction.*

It is astounding to learn how many steps of meiosis the female mammalian ovary carries out before it has even created an egg. Before birth, in the womb of the mother, a daughter's ovaries are already sorting and selecting germ cells and carrying out a form of meiosis, which it then suspends until puberty. To be clear, this happens within the womb of the mother before the girl baby is even born. These suspended germ cells are called the "primary oocytes."

As a girl begins to ovulate each month, these suspended cells become active again. During the follicular phase of a fertile woman's cycle (the first half of her moon cycle before ovulation), meiosis occurs two times. The process of meiosis carried out in the ovary and oocyte is much more complex that I had been led to believe, and seems to be intimately involved with the cyclical, rhythmical timing of our body "clocks."

This process of meiosis, which is completed at the time of fertilization, has begun and been suspended three times by the ovary before it reaches that point.[41] And the suspension begins in the ovaries of a fetus! How amazing is that? How does a cell know to "suspend"? And how precise must this all be in order for reproduction to occur?

There is also a connection between the ovaries and melatonin. Melatonin—a hormone that is connected to our circadian rhythms, and was previously thought to only be synthesized in the pineal gland in the center of our brains—is now thought to also be synthesized in the ovaries. Melatonin has been shown to have a direct relationship to ovaries and to the process of meiosis. There is a lot of melatonin within the mature follicle. Is the melatonin a factor in signaling the cell to suspend? Is melatonin our body clock's information molecule? A timing hormone?

The Serpent and the Egg

What about the snake, traveling across these eggs, seeming to spark them to life?

All forms of life on the planet are in deep connection with the Earth's magnetic field, especially our reproductive, endocrine, central nervous system, and immune system. The planet has a pulse, a heartbeat so to speak; an Earthbeat. It is a very low-level electromagnetic rhythm that our bodies are synchronized with.

The Earth's large magnetic field is generated from its iron and nickel core. This field acts as a sort of shield protecting Earth from oncoming loose dirt and debris in the cosmos. Without the magnetic field, biological life would not have formed on Earth.

The human body possesses an ancient analog system of direct-current energy, which responds to the Earth's field. The electromagnetic pulsations of our brains match those of the Earth. These are very low-level, electromagnetic pulsations that our bodies sense and stay in rhythm with.[42] As much as our bodies are tuned into the dark/light 24-hour circadian rhythm, they are also aligned to the daily electromagnetic rhythm. The analog system in our bodies receives messages from the electromagnetic fields it encounters. (For more on this subject see Appendix B on electromagnetism located in this book.)

103

Is the snake on these Cucuteni images a representation of the electromagnetic pulse of the planet? Electromagnetism is directly involved in fertility and reproduction because it is directly related to our rhythms and timing — our "biocycles." Our bodies derive information from the electromagnetic messages they receive. The pituitary and hypothalamus glands — which send timing messages to the ovaries — are two centers in the brain that are in direct communication with the electromagnetic fields.[43]

The electromagnetic field of the planet is connected to cell division as well. It is the timing, the rhythm, the wave of communication that inspires the cell to divide, the egg to split, life to form.

Because Earth is in close relationship to the moon and the sun, the pulse of the planet is most affected by their cycles. The cycling of the moon affects the pulse of the planet and the rhythms in the life systems it houses.

Earth's magnetic field also appears to be in relationship, albeit not fully understood, with the pineal gland and the melatonin it releases. The production of pineal melatonin, our timekeeping hormone, is affected by electromagnetic fields.

Ancient Wisdom

Because ancient people had no artificial electromagnetism in their environment, they were surely in intimate relationship with the pulse of the planet. We marvel at the fact that ancient stone temples, pyramids, and stone circles align with the phases of the sun and moon and their relationship to Earth. Is the monthly and seasonal change and fluctuation in the Earth's electromagnetic field an unexplored motive in this? Electromagnetic fields are cut off during an eclipse. Is this the reason why eclipses were viewed as dangerous by so many cultures? Is this why there were often rituals carried out at these moments? Did they understand that the propagation of life on Earth depends on the resonance between biocycles and the Earthbeat?

The One that is the All

In sacred geometry, original unity is **One**. The origin, original number of all, is one complete circle. The circle is one. One is the beginning. One is unity with all. **Two** can only emerge from the one and only from the one dividing itself into the two (mitosis). In this cosmology, two can never be separate, as they have arisen from the one—original unity creates them. They are two parts of unity yet whole unto themselves.

Two is the portal through which can arise **Three** (meiosis). From three, all subsequent numbers are born. **Three**: portal to the multiplicity, the many, the masses.

The moon—one whole—does math in the sky by dividing herself and adding back to herself each cycle. Early people used the moon to understand math. Addition, division, subtraction, multiplication—it all takes place in the nighttime sky. Linear time was organized and understood through lunar cycles. Egyptian math was a series of divisions of the one, creating the multiple. Women's bodies are clearly in intimate connection with this cycling.

The Cucuteni eggs can be considered in this way: original unity giving rise to two, and so on and so on. Mitosis and meiosis can be seen in this way as well. Inside a women's ovaries the story of the creation is repeated during each monthly cycling with the moon. The moon instructs and oversees this process on Earth. Its cycle and the follicular cycle on the ovaries of mammals are fractals of this larger whole.

Let's imagine the Cucuteni artists knew about cell division

105

as a function of regeneration and its relationship to the moon. Lets say they understood it and devoted time and energy to honoring it in their temples and shrines. It is a worthy thing to honor, to represent. Why not? I can think of many lesser things that we honor these days. Why not honor the cycle of cosmic creation held within the double eggs of female bodies on Earth and mediated by the moon?

Can we imagine what it would be like to do this?

Once you know something and honor it, you may begin to participate with it. Perhaps it is time to bring this knowing back to active consciousness once again.

Conclusion

Please Feed the Wedeme

I hope some of the information presented in this book helps you navigate your spiritual journey in whatever form it takes for you. Being in communication with beings in other realms is a great gift and an enriched way to live. Working directly with local land, mountains, and waterways can ground and center you in ways nothing else will. Dedicating some of your time and energy to deep listening is a way to walk more gently on this planet.

Most of the preceding information has come through the wedeme and the relationship that was forged with them through my initiation into stick divination, and my continued work with them in that modality.

The wedeme work hard. My wish is that if you have received any gifts from the previous pages, you acknowledge their part in it by feeding them. You may feed them with food or spirits left in a special place for them, or coins offered on the mountain or into the water. You may also light a candle with an intention and prayer for them. Please follow whatever your heart guides you to do.

These small beings with huge hearts truly miss us. And, if you have not already, once you begin to interact with them, you may feel how much you have been missing them.

With deepest gratitude and appreciation, I wish you well on your continuing journey.

Appendices

Appendix A

Source Energy
The Archetype of the Womb

Part I: Containers of Safety

Once there was the archetype of a nurturing womb that lived in the collective human psyche, offering comfort and assurance. This archetype was a strong and persistent one. Modern Westerners have lost this archetype. The loss of this powerful archetype leaves us with many wounds: a deep sense of isolation, alienation, disconnection, and disorientation. We are plagued and haunted by deep, primal fear. This fear drives us, continually leading us in the wrong direction, away from a return to the *Archetype of the Womb*.

The *Archetype of the Womb*, the number one in sacred geometry, is one of connectedness, interconnectedness, unity, and community. There is a birth from and return to the nurturing womb, rendering blood and darkness a sacred mystery. The mystery is held within the womb. When the Universe, *kosmos*, is viewed as a womb, there is the awareness of a series of nested wombs held within this larger womb image—an infinite nesting of wombs within wombs. Carefully held contained space creates more carefully held contained space.

The Universal womb enables the galactic womb, solar system womb, solar and Earth womb, ocean womb, community and village womb, mother womb, daughter womb, cellular and quantum womb.

When this archetype has a living presence, there is an organic feeling of belonging—a constant and reliable place to return to, release to, dissolve or melt into. The womb is the place of birth and death; the before, during, and the after. There is a deep trust in knowing that the womb space holds us all—all life, all systems, all realities. There is no outside. All are held within.

There is the story of Seth, the god who holds the negative or opposing force in Egyptian tradition, breaking through his mother's womb with his impatience to be born. Perhaps this is the definition of evil: breaking this precious held space; breaking the web of connectedness and then believing that the broken web is the truth.

The loss of the *Archetype of the Womb* has led to a loss and devaluation of mothering energy, mothering presence, and mothers in general. I doubt any of us know what mothering energy looks like in its purest form. There are so many overlays and projections, mostly negative. Pure mother energy has fierce boundaries. We see this in the animal world. Mothers are not "nice" among birds and bears. Mothers get the job done and the main job of a mother is protection. Many human mothers in the Western world feel powerless to protect their children; rather, mothering is the experience of a slow inculcation and preparation of our young to accept the realities of life in a world of horror.

I believe if the *Archetype of the Womb* were present, there would be no global warming, humans would not be killing species at record rates, and there would be no war. To the mother energy who knows what it takes — the time and energy to create — life is too precious to squander. Pure mother energy also knows how each and every manifestation of life is unique, special, and essential to the whole. Pure mother energy does not need to arise only from mothers and females, but it is always a female energy.

The *Archetype of the Womb* is that of the container — contained space, the alchemical space within which transmutation occurs. Within this womb container all arises, transmutes, becomes, and dissolves back into the cauldron of the womb to arise yet again, again transformed, again becoming, again dissolving. A wise woman once said to me life is about transforming matter. When you are down, depressed, feeling lost, go and make something. You'll feel better. Why? Because you will be participating with the Universe in its ultimate purpose.

We Westerners envision ourselves as sitting on the outside of an unprotected planet in a dangerous solar system within a meaningless Universe. Because of this, we feel acutely alone, at risk, and profoundly vulnerable, but this is not the truth of our existence.

We are held within countless containers of safety. The Earth, our mother, created a variety of systems to enclose us within layers of protection while remaining interactive with our local solar system. The atmosphere and magnetosphere are but two examples of systems created by the Earth that repel asteroids and other space debris, as well as harmful radiation, while allowing other beneficial matter and light in. Similarly, the heliosphere of the sun encloses and holds the solar system within a contained, protected space while interacting with the galaxy as a whole, and so on. Layer upon layer of membranes that are permeable, yet protective. This more accurately describes the truth of our existence.

113

As stated previously in this book, cosmologist Brian Swimme cites the emergence of the membrane as one of the most crucial developments for the presence of life on Earth. "Really dynamic creative emergence requires isolation, removal, separation in order to articulate itself. The membrane protects complexity and creative power."[44] I see the membrane as but another manifestation of the *Archetype of the Womb*. It is a womb that folds around that which has been created, to preserve and protect it, like a mother's arms.

If you believed you were held in a within space that you shared with all the rest of life as you know it, would you consider differently how to behave?

We have lost the understanding of Source Energy, the *Archetype of Connectedness*.

The physical manifestations of the loss of this archetype are everywhere around us. Losing this archetype has allowed us to destroy permeable yet protective membranes. Here we are able to see how the state of our psyches directly affects physical matter. We are destroying the atmosphere, one of the layers of the womb, because we do not believe in it. Because we do not believe in it, we are losing it; we are allowing it to be destroyed. We are creating what we believe deeply. We are literally creating the reality of disconnection and alienation that we carry deep in our psyches.

This *Archetype of the Womb* has had many manifestations in human consciousness. Around 10,000 BCE it arose in the human psyche in the form of *bucrania* (bull head and horns). Throughout the Middle East at this time period, archaeologists begin to find the skulls and horns of wild bulls and cows buried underneath housing, embedded inside the plaster of the walls and benches, and used as a decorative motif in association with images of the Goddess. They call this image "the bull" and "male," and mostly separate it from the

114

Goddess images. But it is not separate and it is not male. It is yet another image of the Goddess. It is the womb of the Goddess. These bucranium are images of the horned cow, the Cow Goddess, which is a manifestation of the *Archetype of the Womb*.

African Hathor is a Cow Goddess. From her udders flow the milk that creates and sustains life in the cosmos. Hathor is the Goddess of Papyrus, the opener of wombs, Goddess of Love, the Mother. She is the goddess of licentiousness, ecstasy. She is also associated with the sistrum, a tambourine-type percussion instrument. Her priestesses were dancers and musicians. Her celebrations were bawdy and sexual. She is Mistress of the Vulva. Wooden phalluses were left to her.

Hathor means "house of Horus"; her womb housed Horus. Horus is the level of transmutation humans aspired to in Egypt and in alchemical traditions. You need the womb within which to be transmuted. No matter how "enlightened" someone is or a tradition is, if they miss the boat on this one, it is no good. Nothing happens in isolation. No one transforms oneself — the container of your life, beliefs, and experiences transforms you. And this is held female space. We are destroying the womb container of the Earth. Global warming is nothing other than this. If we destroy the container, nothing can live, meaning nothing can transform. Womb space is generated at the core, then emanates out and around. Womb space comes from within the within; a deeply interior space that creates new, deeply interior space.

Hathor is a solar Goddess. If life on Earth is transformed sunlight, she is the transformer — the one who holds the space within which transmutation occurs; the vessel, container, womb. She is often depicted as a vessel. She wears a sun disc on her head between her horns. Her symbol is the mirror, which captures the sun within it and transmutes it, a reflection of the sun, herself reflecting and channeling sun. She is a Sky Goddess, often associated with Nut. She is the mother Goddess, the nurturing womb archetype.

It was Dorothy Cameron who originally pointed out that the bucrania image, so omnipresent in the cultures that worshiped the Goddess in prehistory, is a perfect replica of a human woman's uterus, fallopian tubes, and ovaries.[45]

We know that ancient people knew human anatomy because they engaged in the process of excarnation. Excarnation is a process where the bodies of the recently dead were left out in the open air to be exposed to the elements— sun, wind, rain, and vultures—their flesh offered up as food. The priest/priestess carrying out the service would have observed the internal organs at certain stages of decomposition; they would have seen the female reproductive organs in various stages of pregnancy. The flesh they offered to the vultures, the sun, the wind, and the air for further transmutation. The cleaned and bleached bones they carried back to their shrines or temples, placed them into clay pots or baskets, and buried them under the floors of their houses. Undoubtedly, there were rituals involving the bucrania that invoked returning them, in the form of their cleaned and prepared bones, to the womb of the Goddess for rebirth.

Bucrania images were often created out of plaster with actual horns. These carefully crafted images protruded from walls of tomb-like spaces, and adorned alters or the ends of benches. They were painted onto pots and clay vessels as well. Later, the image is stylized into the downward-facing triangle. The Egyptian hieroglyph for uterus is **V**.

Barbara G. Walker writes, "Perhaps the most common manifestation of the Great Mother as Preserver was the white, horned, milk-giving Moon-cow, still sacred in India as a symbol of Kali."[46] As Lat, Al-lat, Latona, Lado, Leto, or Leda, she was known as the "milk giver"; Io, Europa, Hera, Brigid, horned-cow Goddesses all. Cow as Creatrix. In shrines uncovered in the Neolithic village of Çatal Hüyük (circa 7th mill. BCE) located in what is now Turkey, we find bucranium lining the walls, or protruding from walls underneath painted images of the large, spreading wings of vultures, being born from between the legs of the awesome frog Goddess. From Prehistoric Crete are images of bucrania and bulls, often with a labrys (double axe) symbol of cyclical nature of life/death nonduality in its head. In Sardinia (circa 4th mill. BCE) in underground, egg-shaped tombs, images of bucrania hang over doors and entryways, as well as emerge from and line the circular walls within as a recurring, repeating symbol.

In an astounding image from Egypt in Saqqara—the cemetery site for early dynastic Memphis (3100-2800 BCE) 300 Bucrania surround tomb #3504, excavated by Emery. The heads are made of mud, but the horns are genuine. They must have collected them for some time. These 300 line perfectly the outer wall of the tomb complex. It is a powerful image. The idea of rebirth within the womb of the Goddess exists long before this, and worship of Hathor has a powerful and central presence in Egypt at this time, and yet in written descriptions of the tomb I find only references to the bull and the kingship. As stated previously in this book, in West Africa, she is Nyame.

Hathor is mistress of the West. The Netherworld was located in the West. She was well known for her ability to revive the dead. She greets the dead with food to sustain them on their journey. Why is this left out of the interpretation of the 300 bucrania surrounding a tomb in early Egypt?

Hathor is a midwife. She is present at birth; she is the opener of wombs; she is the one to go to when one needs help with fertility, sexuality. She is a healer. The active presence of this archetype gives way for physical human manifestations that will embody the archetype. Hathor, as a midwife Goddess, a healer and sage, gives way to the wise woman, the midwife, the Strega, the Curandera, the witch. Without her, there is no place for these kinds of women. Without her, women who embody these particular powers become frightening aberrations.

The swallow is the sacred animal of Hathor. Swallows are associated with the sun and fire. Contrary to most recent Goddess scholarship, which places male energy firmly with the sun and female with the moon, the Goddesses of Egypt are mostly sun Goddesses. Osiris is the Moon God, who dies and is resurrected. In the Mideast there was the tradition of the sun Goddess and her consort Moon God husband/lover/son, who died and resurrected like the moon on a monthly basis. Some say the story of Jesus was yet a continuation of this; the Moon God who was sacrificed ritually to ensure fertility and everlasting life.

Studying the Egyptian pantheon does not allow one to make definitive statements. There is an ambiguity, an overlapping, a changeability to their Goddesses and Gods that can be confusing, but also instructional, especially for us Westerners with our often black-and-white view of the world. The Gods and Goddesses of Egypt inhabit the meaning of both. They exchange roles, names; they are at once animals, symbols, words, and opposing energies. At different times they are different elements.

One reason for this is the long time span documented of Egyptian belief. Changes in belief are mirrored in the changing roles of Goddesses and Gods. However, this changeability is also indicative of the nondual view of life that the Egyptians held, which is also revealed in their views on evil. Things were not evil as in bad or wrong, they were in opposition. They were twins, another part of the totality or whole, another side, another aspect. They embodied energies we now label as evil, but I do not believe the Egyptians saw it that way. These energies are what we now call "the shadow," the repressed and cut-off parts of ourselves, but they were not shadows in Egyptian belief. They were out in the open, and they were revered. They were powers humans had access to.

With this in mind, it is important to move to the other aspect of Hathor, our womb Goddess, lest we get wrapped up in modern views of mother energy as only a nurturing force. Hathor is another manifestation of Sekhmet, her twin or dual/nondual aspect, and Sekhmet is the fierce Goddess in Egypt. She is a lion, fire, what some would call a destroyer Goddess — the destructive side of creation, but also, like Kali, the one who cuts through illusion to truth — the one who will kill you and cut you down to protect that which she loves, which is nothing less than all of life itself.

Like Durga, the fierce Hindu Goddess who rides a lion, she is a bloodthirsty Goddess. In fact, Sekhmet's story is very similar to Durga's in that she is invoked to clean up the Earth when things are out of control, and that this involves the drinking of blood. Sekhmet has been given the task of destroying humans who have forgotten about Ra. Her force becomes uncontrollable once unleashed and it seems all of humanity will be destroyed. She is reined in through drinking pomegranate juice laced with beer, which she, thinking it is blood, laps up eagerly, becoming drunk and passing out.

And yet the Sekhmet in this story, the fierce murderous Goddess to be feared, is only one facet of this powerful lion. There is so much more to this Goddess that has been overlooked, most evident in the fact that she is the dual aspect of Hathor, the nurturing mother womb. Like the womb itself, with its ability to carry and create life as well as its ability to bleed and destroy life, to Hathor's sparrow is Sekhmet's lion.

The womb is awash with life-giving blood.

Sekhmet's name means "The Powerful One." She is the "dynamo of Divine Light, the energy that drives the universe."[47] She too wears the sun disc on her head. The lion's face is a reflection of the sun. Don't get too close to either.

Intriguing to me is the fact that Sekhmet derives her name from the word *sekhem.* In *Dreams of Isis,* Normandi Ellis tells of being in the temple of Edfu and seeing an image of a lion-headed serpent, tongue thrust forward between her teeth, "Buddha-like."

"She is the goddess of the life-force herself—Sekhmet. She is the fire that arises up in all things the way a flame leaps to a bit of wood to consume it, or the way life essence shoots up through the ground each spring."[48]

Sekhem is the life force, the *kundalini,* the *numen, chi.* Ellis tells us sekhem literally means "the powers." Sekhem is the life force generated in and rising out of the womb space. Mother is life force, creatrix/destroyer. This is not a passive force—a subservient, patient force. This is the magic that moves through beings and enlivens them. Mother = life energy. And life energy is a blade that cuts both ways.

If Hathor is pregnancy and birth, Sekhmet is menstruation, menopause, and puberty; the woman raging on hormones, the woman who needs some space. In our so-called *modern* world, she is the madwoman, the shadowed and split-off part.

Female lions are the hunters in that species. They know how to take care of themselves and their young. They understand protection. What is the big mystery of the Sphinx? If you were the pharaoh, would you choose anyone other to be your protectress in the afterworld? This is an awesome power and it is held in the womb matrix—the archetype of the self-contained, self-creating universe. This is the part of woman, womb, mother that Christianity and so many Western religions left out, and why women are so conflicted and split, disconnected. Sekhmet is no "nice girl." She is no doormat. Her boundaries are clear. The *Archetype of the Womb* is a powerhouse of creativity. Sekhmet. We have a lion in our wombs. No one ever told me that, but I knew it all the while. I experience her red liquid every moon.

Sekhmet is associated and depicted with the color red. She is called the "scarlet lady." She is Lilith of the Red Sea; Inanna, the whore; Magdalene of the red hair and red dress. She is blood. We "see red" when we are angry. We are angry when our boundaries are violated. Sekhmet is the protective boundary of the membrane, saying "No!" We see the Hathor/Sekhmet dual/nondual nature repeated over and over again in the Eve/Lilith, Virgin Mary/Mary Magdalene relationships, to name only a couple.

Creation and destruction are dual aspects of this same archetypal energy. Revering and honoring destructive power is a way of being in relationship with it rather than hoping that by denying it, it will go away. We must dance with the fires of creativity, we must die to be reborn, we must cut through our egoic tendencies to accomplish any real work on ourselves. In the container of the womb it is the fire, the heat, which transforms.

This dual power is the womb and it holds us all. Even in death we are yet held by the womb. Since there is no outside, all is eternally present. With the presence of Sekhmet in the *Archetype of the Womb,* death is not bad, other, or an unexplainable horror. Death (not gratuitous violence, not war, not out-of-control rage) is essential to life. It is a gift. The dead are ever present (there is nowhere else to go). Within the womb container, death is the ultimate transformation. Ancient and indigenous people understand this. The ancestors are interacted with, held close for the good of the living. Death is a realm, not an ending.

If our psyches held the *Archetype of the Womb*, all aspects of it, would there be less confusion? If we honored the archetypal power of Sekhmet, would we be less inclined to rail against it? Egyptians, fearful Sekhmet would go on the attack again, were pious in honoring her. There was the belief that destructive forces can be riled or kept in line through human actions.

Restoring the *Archetype of the Womb* to human consciousness could do a lot toward restoring harmony on Earth.

Source Energy
The Archetype of the Womb

Part II : Womb Ovens

ascinating artifacts depicting beliefs about the *Archetype of the Womb* are bread ovens created in the shape of a pregnant human uterus; images of female hips as wide, encircling alchemical ovens, and temples of worship that contain bread ovens as a focal point.

In the Neolithic Cucuteni Culture of Eastern Europe we find profound illustrations of this concept. The Cucuteni Culture (circa 4800-3500 BCE), located in areas of Romania, Russia, where it is called Tripolye and Ukraine (Trypillia) was a prepatriarchal culture that grew to enormous size and left a wealth of artifacts. Their ceramic pottery and designs are among the most elegant in human prehistory.

The largest Cucuteni village, Tal'noe, south of present-day Kiev, had up to 20,000 people and 1,500 houses on 700 acres.[49] Here, the earliest cultivation of cherry trees is found, as well as other orchards of fruit and fields of cultivated grains. They raised cattle and pigs and engaged in hunting and fishing. Cucuteni villages were often circular, with the tallest buildings positioned at the outer ring for protection from wild animals, and a meeting place at the village center.

Cucuteni villagers lived in rectangular houses with two or three rooms and containing a large hearth and separate bread oven. There were many two-story buildings; some of these were ceramic workshops, with ceramics stored on the top floor, and a work area with kilns below. In one of these workshops archaeologists discovered an early version of a pottery wheel, and one of the first two-tiered ovens for baking earthenware. Burials of women with pottery tools were uncovered and all depictions of people creating pottery were female. It may be that this was a female craft.

Within the Shrine of the Bread Goddess

〜〜〜 〜〜〜 〜〜〜

What does it mean to bake bread in worship? What does it mean to bake bread as worship to Her? To bake bread in the many shapes and manifestations of Her? To bake bread in adoration of Her regenerative womb?

What would it be like to gather together to roll and shape dough into female forms, the uncooked dough sticking to your fingers as you shape it into the likeness of Her nurturing womb space. As your hands shape warm dough into rounded loaves, the ripe and potent dough pushes against your fingers — responds. You stamp the bread dough with a symbol of regeneration. Spiral, seeded triangle, meander: symbols of moving energy, transformation, sacred process of the Goddess.

Imagine the shrine, a large central oven fired by wood felled by your axes, carried by your arms, stacked by your hands in the process of clearing trees to maintain the health of the forest, your immediate neighborhood, your ecosystem, your village; the firewood itself and the fire created from it yet another manifestation of the alchemical process of the Universe.

Can you feel the warmth of the shrine room where dough is rising, where bread is baking, your body hot on the inside? Can you smell the rich dough baking, transforming, becoming? This is not a sit-down-and-be-quiet kind of church; in this temple activity is taking place. I imagine low humming, group singing, quiet conversation about people in need. Soft prayer is being spoken. Perhaps someone has an instrument, a drum. There could be slight dancing, hips moving with the beat. You grind grain that you have planted and sown from seed you collected from previous seasons of your own labor. You are witness to this whole process. Bread is the ultimate outcome, is the culmination: food. Eating the bread is the reward — pleasure and engaged participation in the creative process of the Universe. I want to go to this church!

~~~ ~~~ ~~~

I believe that early people had an intuitive, if not more informed, way of knowing that the process that turns galactic clouds into stars, births planets and lifeforms, is the same one that turns grass that starts from a seed into edible, warm, velvety bread. It is the alchemical process of the Universe, which they envisioned as the Goddess. The alchemical process of baking bread, molding and heating clay into pots, metallurgy, weaving, horticulture, giving birth — these are all ways of participating with that process. Early people understood this, and so they baked bread to honor the force they saw as responsible for the universal process of becoming. They saw this force as female. How do we know they envisioned Her as a Goddess, a female force? Because they baked images of female in clay, because they created temple models with breasts, because they created ovens in the shape of the human uterus.

Baking bread in ritual fashion is a custom well known in European cultures, where it is a continuous tradition still active today. We are sure that ancient Goddess worshippers carried on this practice, for there is a reference in the bible to the pagan

125

women who baked bread (cakes) to the *Queen of Heaven*.

In *Dreams of Isis*, Normandi Ellis tells us that in Egypt, "hieroglyphically, all goddesses are indicated by the *t* phonetic sign, which was the image of a loaf of bread, and that the ancient Egyptian bread of heaven was originally the Goddess Nut."[50] Nut is the Sky Goddess who swallows the sun, Ra, every night to be reborn through her body into the morning. Each night Ra is transformed within the body of the Goddess, traveling through her interior darkness, birthed back into the light. Here again is evidence of sacred eating, being "devoured" by the Goddess, coexisting with ideas of death and rebirth — transformation.

In my own Italian-American tradition, my grandmother baked bread ritually every Easter, creating what she called an "Easter baby" with an egg in its center. Curiously, the "baby" always had large breasts. This was no baby.

Many Goddesses in all cultures are associated with grain: Demeter (Greek), Ceres & Annona (Roman), Ukemochi (Japanese), Quinoa-Mama (Peru), Zaramama (Peruvian corn goddess). The most famous Goddess image from Çatal Hüyük, a Neolithic village in Anatolia, large-bellied and seated between two lions, was found in a grain bin.

Clay stamps have been found in the shape of loaves. These were probably stamped onto the top of the bread either before baking or when it came out of the oven. The symbols on the stamps are often spirals, seeded lozenges, meanders and labyrinths; symbols identified with regeneration.[51]

One bread oven found in Hungary (circa 5000 BCE) has the shape of a pregnant human uterus with an umbilical cord on the top. The oven is marked with energetic lines.[52] Could these be contractions?

The Neolithic revolution, which brought about a more settled lifestyle and the development of the cultivation of crops, gave rise to the conscious awareness of this transformative force that humans found they could participate with in ways before unknown. In the Cucuteni Culture (Trilpolye/Trypillia) of Eastern Europe, predating Dynastic Egypt, we find potent illustration of this consciousness arising in humans and the sacred ritual they used to honor it.

Archaeological Indications

From Popudnia, in Western Ukraine, north of Uman, there is a Cucuteni model of a shrine with the bread oven as the focal point. In this truly astounding shrine model, not only is the baking honored, but the process of grinding the wheat into flour as well. On the bench to the right of the oven was found a female figurine with her hands on her breasts. There is another sculpture on the far side of a woman grinding grain. There are pear-shaped vases on a platform, perhaps for grain storage, offerings, or yet another metaphor for the womb. In the middle of the room is a "raised platform in the shape of a cross decorated with grooves ... such cross shaped platforms also occur in the actual houses of the Cucuteni settlements and are known to be places for votive offerings."[53] The shrine has a separate entryway and a threshold over which one must cross to enter. One wonders who was allowed in this special place.

The posture of a woman with her hands on her breasts is a prevalent one throughout cultures that honored the Goddess. It is an honoring of the sacred life force that moves through a woman's breasts upon pregnancy and nursing her young. The Goddess not only births you and takes you back when you die, but sustains you through life with her nourishment. This is a sacred act, this gesture of putting one's hands to one's breasts. It is a gesture saying "I recognize and honor the Goddess within." Did it incorporate a slight bow? Here we have the

127

Goddess being honored as the universal nurturing force in combination with a shrine to the Bread Goddess. Eating bread baked within the context of these shrines is yet another ritual honoring the transformational process of the Universe; eating, yet another part of this process, an act of transmutation.

In the early Cucuteni settlement of Sabatinovka II in Western Ukraine, we find a full-scale temple with an oven as the focal point, dating from 4800-4600 BCE. Covering most of the far wall is a long bench altar. Next to the altar is an oversized, horned seat. Wide-hipped, female figurines are found on the stone steps of the entryway, inside by the oven and on the altar where 16 sit within horned chairs, mirroring the life-sized one beside them. I wonder over these chairs. Were they birthing chairs? Initiation chairs? Clearly Hathor, the horned Cow Goddess, is also in this room. Some of the figurines hold baby snakes in their arms. They sit upon wide, egg-shaped hips and buttocks, which are accentuated and match the recurring theme of the culture that crafted their female figurines with emphasis on the womb center. If we were to crack open these hips, would there be eggs held within them, as with other sculptures in this culture?

A human woman probably sat in this chair, but to what purpose? Unfortunately, this horned chair is often called a throne. The word "throne" is problematic in that it implies a style of hierarchy — pomp and circumstance, power over — which I do not believe early people engaged in. Possibly a wise woman or a priestess sat in this chair to carry out a ritual. I believe it was a chair that every woman sat in at certain transitional stages of her cyclic female life. The chair is a meter wide and originally had split planks covering it.[54] One meter is large, especially for a time when people were smaller. Perhaps more than one person sat here at a time; mother, daughter, sisters, maiden friends, crone friends, a large pregnant woman.

128

Was this a chair to bless the microcosm of the universal alchemical womb held within each individual female's hips, and all the power that implies?

The large-hipped women signify the ability to generate, regenerate, to transform; her hips yet another metaphor for the oven, the alchemical urn; the oven yet a metaphor for her hips. One wonders whether bread was baked in a similar shape to these wide-hipped, fat-thighed women, then offered up and eaten in ritual fashion.

When people speak of "fertility Goddesses" many go directly to the process of birth and reproduction, to *insemination*. The honoring of "fertility" is so much more. It is a complex honoring of the life process of generation, death, regeneration, becoming, dissolving, and becoming again. This includes honoring ovulation, and the absolute magic of the process carried out by the human female ovaries every moon, itself a cyclical process of generation, death, and rebirth. Honoring fertility includes an honoring of the *Archetype of the Womb*, which includes the uterus, fallopian tubes, and ovaries. The "horns" are the fallopian tubes and ovaries. The *Archetype of the Womb* includes all of these components of a woman's womb center. The *Archetype of the Womb* is horned — or, as I like to refer to it, "winged"; the fallopian tubes and ovaries are that which allow it to "take flight."

The female sculptures found in the remains of this culture are particularly provocative and tie into the overall cosmology of these people, which was very much concerned with the generative force of the Universe as embodied in the female form. They are large-hipped women with the top portion of the body de-emphasized. Frequently, the buttocks protrude backward as though the woman is thrusting them out to add even more emphasis, in case we missed the point, which we clearly have for over 2,000 years.

The figurines are marked with various symbols. Energy lines run up and down the body, opposing spirals spin and whirl at the place of the back of the hips, and a large, elongated spiral moves and swirls over the breasts, as though to accentuate the sustaining and nourishing energy found there. These markings honor and represent forces moving within the woman, within her body, and within the body of the Goddess. I use the word "within" because when found, some of these figurines were broken open, revealing within the hip space two neatly nestled eggs. Double-egg images abound in this culture, painted onto vessels and onto the base of large plates and platters. Double eggs within the hips as in, "within her hips there were eggs baking."

Often I think these Goddesses are images of the *body of the Universe*, and the markings indications of the creative power in the cosmos. Like Nut, She *is* the cosmos; the stars live upon her skin. Some have interpreted these markings as tattoos the actual Cucuteni women had on their bodies. What are these "energy lines"? Even if they were tattoos, they had to be representative of something. They could be indicative of hormonal changes a woman's body goes through every month, and then extremely at puberty and menopause. Interestingly, hormonal changes in a woman are primarily orchestrated by the ovaries, the dual eggs nestled within her hip center. Perhaps Cucuteni sculptors understood on a fundamental level the power of the hormones created by the ovaries, and the energy patterns generated and moving out from the dual eggs at women's cores.

Herbalist Susun Weed sees the "energy lines" as exact depictions of menopausal hot flash energy, which she calls a *kundalini* awakening. Kundalini is the term Hindus give to the energy of the serpent of the base of the spine waiting to be awakened. The awakening of this serpent leads to

130

enlightenment. In the shrine of Sabatinovka II, some of the figurines on the altar were holding "baby" serpents. It is increasingly clear that the kundalini force in a woman lives in the uterus and ovaries, rather than at the base of the spine as is always suggested. It is often orchestrated by the female hormones, of which the ovaries are main producers. Women have spontaneous kundalini experiences at birth, puberty, and menopause; times of intense hormonal activity. Kundalini is a natural part of a woman's body chemistry, not something we need to strive for or "achieve." Ancient women knew this. Kundalini has been called many things by different cultures: *sekhem, numen, chi*, serpent of fire, life force. Kundalini permeates the cosmos and also a woman's womb center within the furnace of her nurturing hips; fire, heat, the heat which transforms, the womb and ovaries as the internal oven-transformer-generator.

Are these shrines and wide-hipped women a depiction of the oven/generator at our cores, literally heating things up and "baking" us, getting things "cooking"? The ovaries and uterus are the storehouse and generator of kundalini energy, the energy of enlightenment. Our ovaries and wombs within are transmutational centers. Cucuteni people also worked in metallurgy; they understood the fire which transforms. They saw that this "serpent energy" is generated at our cores. They knew that women carry the *Holy Grail* within their hips.

Women embody the alchemical womb oven of the Goddess at all times, whether or not we are still fertile and bleeding, whether or not we have had a hysterectomy. The power center is still there. We are microcosms of the *Archetype of the Womb*. We hold this power within us. It sits at our centers, these days largely ignored and unappreciated, or even hated and reviled. The truth is, the Goddess created us in *Her* image. Ancient women, Cucuteni women, and our ancestresses, honored this knowing in their shrines and with their womb ovens. The imagery they left behind, the language and markings, the art and the passion these artifacts still palpably emit almost 7,000 years later, can lead us back to this knowing. Thank you, Cucuteni Mothers of the past.

When the bread is baked we gather together and eat Her, Her body nurturing our bodies that we may feed other bodies, transforming us that we may in turn transform.

Appendix B

Electromagnetism: A Circuitous, Nonlinear Affair

I f you wander into scientific theory on any topic, it can seem a bit elusive. That is because scientific theories are developed to elucidate *behavior* that is exhibited, while the *cause* is not often understood. It is important for a layperson to understand that at the root of science in general resides mystery. Take electromagnetism for instance. Electromagnetism is a fundamental part of both the Universe and our daily lives. It powers our household electronics, cell phones, and computers, yet most people have no idea what it is, how it works, and whether it could possibly affect our health. Part of the confusion may be due to the fact that, like science in general, at the root of electromagnetism exists a mystery; something not understood or explained.

The fundamental mystery of electromagnetism is *charge*. Magnetic fields are created by electricity. Electricity is created by *charge* and *charge* is not understood.[55] *Charge* simply *is*. Electromagnetism, or waves of electrical *charge*, is a part of our environment—the organism of Earth to which we belong. This is true whether it is naturally occurring (electromagnetism that is created by Earth and its many life forms) or human created (that which we create to run our technology – electromagnetic pollution).

Imagine yourself in the center of Earth, in a womb-like space, in total darkness. What sounds and feels like the steady beating of a drum is coming from this warm, dark core. The waves emanating from this drumbeat wash over you, and your being begins to beat in time with it. It is a primal beat, a pulse of waves keeping you alive. You are reminded of being within the body of your mother before you were born, and being in intimate connection with the rhythmic beating of her heart. This electromagnetic pulsation is your umbilical cord to Earth.

Our planet has a beat, an Earth beat; a very low-level electromagnetic rhythm that its lifesystems have evolved with and are synchronized with. Studies have shown that being cut off from this pulse upsets the "clocks" – the rhythms and biocycles a lifesystem uses to regulate itself – in plants, animals, and humans.[56] Earth is an organism, a being, a system, that has, through a process of creativity that took 4.5 billion years, made the space for every lifesystem on the planet to emerge, including the human species. Evolution is a process of interacting with the environment one finds oneself in, and responding, adapting, and aligning. The electromagnetic fields of Earth played a crucial part in the process of the evolution of life on Earth, and continue to inform it at all times.

Mysterious *charge* emerges at both the atomic and subatomic levels. Atoms are made up of electrons and protons, which have opposite *charge*. Atoms can change their *charge* by losing or gaining electrons. This *charge* is randomly termed positive or negative. Opposite *charges* attract each other and repel each other. This is the fundamental basis for electricity. Atoms become *charged* and interact, and waves or particles are

134

created as a result of this *charged* interactive state.[57] Electricity is the movement of electrons—the most moveable components of atoms—and their messenger particles, photons. Electricity creates magnetism and magnetism creates electricity. As it oscillates, this cycle is repeated over and over.

Electricity and magnetism are entirely related and interconnected, thus the term *electromagnetism*. They are two halves of one whole; as interrelated as light is to dark, as yin is to yang, as life is to death. In fact, one could even use the yin/yang symbol as an image of electromagnetism. Imagine them giving birth to each other in a self sustaining cycle of interaction.

Fields are a vital way to begin to conceptualize electromagnetism. An "electromagnetic event," which can be as small as one charged particle or as large as an entire galaxy, is surrounded by a field, which carries information about that event. The field of information emanates out from and around the event in circular waves. These fields perpetuate more fields, the circular lines of information intersecting each other, and these interactions create further perpetuation of themselves and more "electromagnetic events."

An even better image to envision is a web. We are essentially engulfed in a web woven of interacting and intersecting circular fields. Even our bodies, which are electric and magnetic, create fields, and these fields intersect other fields. Information is exchanged and energy transferred and entangled within these webs. The reverberation of the energy transferred depends on the intensity of the *resonance* encountered.

Michael Faraday, the 19th century physicist who proved the existence of electromagnetic fields, called them "strange circles" because they affect objects at a distance in a way no one at the time believed was possible. These omnipresent circular lines, though nonvisible, shape the fabric of the cosmos.

Our planet is an "electromagnetic event" which creates a field called the magnetosphere. The magnetosphere, discovered in 1958 by *Explorer 1*, extends far beyond the atmosphere into the larger solar system. Earth's spinning, molten core of iron and nickel is its "electromagnetic event." This powerful electric *charge* creates this magnetic field around the planet. We are contained and protected from galactic space by this magnetosphere created by Earth. It is the protective womb within which Earth holds us.

We are not wildly unprotected beings on the surface of a vulnerable planet in the middle of cold, unfriendly space. We are cradled within this womb-like field. Earth's field interacts closely with the cycles of the sun and the moon. The electromagnetic field of the sun, the heliosphere, blows against Earth's magnetosphere, causing it to form a tail behind Earth, which trails into space.

The pulsations of the sun's fields affect Earth's magnetosphere. They are in relationship to each other, forming a web-like matrix of interwoven fields. The *heliosphere* is larger, and embraces the entire solar system. Woven together, these pulsing, vibrating fields—Faraday's "strange circles"—enclose us, hold us, surround us.

The Light/Dark Spectrum

The term "electromagnetism" refers to both the visible and nonvisible spectrum; however, all of electromagnetism is habitually called "light." Calling electromagnetism "light" gives the impression that we are speaking only about visible light. It also implies that we should be able to experience all different kinds of electromagnetism the way we experience visible light. This is incorrect and misleading. There are both light and dark forms of electromagnetism. Visible light is one form of electromagnetism—a small range within a spectrum that we are able to see with our eyes. However, there is a larger range of the spectrum that we are *unable* to see with our eyes. These "dark" fields intersect and interact around us. They are invisible, unseen, yet present; webs woven of interacting darkness. X-rays and gamma rays are examples of "dark" electromagnetism, yet they are called "light."

Microwaves are another example of "dark" electromagnetism. We cannot see microwaves, but we allow them to cook our food and power our cell phones. With this technology, we are creating and inviting these electromagnetic fields into our homes and lives in ways never before interacted with by humans and other lifesystems. Though we cannot see "dark" fields with our *eyes*, studies are confirming the fact that other organs of our bodies hear, feel, or sense "dark" electromagnetism with sensitivity equal to how our eyes sense waves of visible light. The pineal gland, the hippocampus, the ovaries, testes, the adrenal glands, and the collective network of our cells are now understood to be acutely sensitive to "dark" fields.[58]

The pineal gland, located in the center of the head, is a gland in the human body that senses and responds to electromagnetism of the visible and nonvisible kind. As master gland of the endocrine system (the system that controls and produces hormones), the pineal gland produces melatonin, the hormone of darkness. Melatonin is a powerful antioxidant and regulates our sleep cycles. It tells our body when it is time to go to sleep and enables our body to sink into a deep sleep—a sleep that includes dreams. Exposure to abnormal electromagnetic fields has been shown to reduce the amount of melatonin the pineal gland produces.[59] The long-term effects of this are unclear. Though we are mostly unaware of it, something as essential as our sleep and our dreaming are related to our body's interaction with the invisible webs of woven darkness. We cannot see the waves signaling us that it is time to sleep, but we obey them nonetheless. In fact, many animals surrender for the whole winter to the influence of these invisible fields.

Photons—The Epitome of Cool

I graduated from college without learning what a photon is. Everyone should know what a photon is, and they should learn about them very early on, because photons are the epitome of cool. In the quantum realm, there are particles that mediate the interactions of the four identified forces: the electromagnetic, gravity, and the strong and weak nuclear forces. The photon is the mediator for electromagnetic interactions. An electromagnetic field is a force field and the photon is the particle carrier, the conveyer of that force. We live in a matrix of photons, which is the electromagnetic field of Earth. A photon is the quanta (the amount of energy that the photon carries) of the electromagnetic interaction.

What does all this mean? Electrons communicate their attraction or repulsion by passing photons back and forth. This relationship is the glue of the electromagnetic interaction. Without electromagnetism, everything would fall apart. Photons act as mediators, keeping electrons connected and carrying information about the interaction that created them. In other words, the photon is the *memory* of that interaction.

Like all quantum particles, a photon can be a particle or a wave. It is, in fact, both. Some have called photons "wavicles." What a cool word! Very appropriate for that which is the epitome of cool. *Wavicles*. It was Einstein who first theorized the existence of photons, a notion rejected for some time by his scientific peers. He described light as a "rain of particles" — more specifically, photons. A rain of wavicles.

138

Photons get to decide on the spot, instantaneously, whether they will be a wave or a particle. Nobody tells a photon what to do. Quantum physics reveals that photons dwell in a timespace of possibility and when they "choose" what it is they want to be, they "collapse" into the chosen form. This collapse is temporary. It is also instantaneously changeable, depending on what happens next. Photons can be either wave or particle, depending on how they are observed, which means that how they are observed affects how they appear. Photons are quantum shamanic shape-shifters.

Another cool factor about photons is that they travel through time and are allowed the highest speed limit in the cosmos, the speed of light.[60] The speed of light is 670 million miles per hour. Take that, Ferrari! As far as we know, there is no faster speed allowed in the universe. This high speed of travel, combined with their infinitesimal mass, also enables them to go right *through* solid objects. Lest you think photons are created and speeding around "out there," remember that *you* are creating them right now! *You* are interacting with them right here and right now. You are full of photons, photonic through and through.

Photons are indeed "wavicles of light," but they are also "wavicles of dark," meaning there are photons we cannot see with our eyes, passing through us right now. There are photons that carry darkness. There are nonvisible photons all around us.

Amplification

The meeting of a photon in the visible light spectrum and a molecule in the human eye sets off a cascade of reactions, which miraculously lead to sight. The process of the retina receiving one photon and the cascade of reactions that follows is possible due to a process called *amplification*. This *amplification* is created by a phenomenon called *coherence*. (We will explore *coherence* in more detail later.) This process, which leads to "sight," illustrates the acute sensitivity the retina has developed for the presence of the photon in the visible light spectrum. It is an interactive relationship that has evolved over millions of years. When the photon wavicle hits the eye, its energy is *amplified* a million times.[61] A million-fold *amplification!*

This type of response requires *resonance*, a synchronous vibration that occurs when an organism has developed the appropriate sensitivity. The presence of "stored energy" enables the *resonance* to be long lasting. If intersecting photonic wavicles share *resonance*, they have the ability to sense and receive each other, to "notice" each other. When the waves are "noticed," energy is exchanged, and functions such as sight occur. This is the definition of intimacy: A developed sensitivity that allows an organism to respond to what is present, to exchange energy, and eventually transmute that energy.[62]

One illustration of such intimacy is between the hippocampus and electromagnetic fields.[63] The hippocampus, located on either side of the temporal lobe, has been called the "transducer of electromagnetic waves."[64] This means it is able to convert electromagnetic messages from the cosmic web into a language the body can understand. The hippocampus is involved with spatial orientation and memory. Many people suffering from depression or Alzheimer's disease are found to have a shrunken or damaged hippocampus.[65] Both of these diseases are epidemic in our culture. Antidepressants are the most commonly prescribed drugs[66] and Alzheimer's is predicted to quadruple in the next 40 years.[67] Recent research by a team in Sweden has shown that the microwave radiation from cell phones causes neural damage to the cortex and hippocampus.[68] Research in the Soviet Union in the 1980s showed similar results.[69] It would be worthwhile to follow this line of research further.

Humans have added an enormous amount of electromagnetic pollution into the spectrum of Earth's field over the past 100 years. The magical heydays of Tesla and Edison started in the 1890s. Once humans figured out how to harness this charge in the atom, when we began to understand the power of electrons, we began to capitalize on it, creating what is now called the electronics industry. Starting with a lowly light bulb, we have transformed into a culture where every house is wired with all kinds of fancy devices. Now wireless, portable, electronic devices that use microwaves and are held close to the body are ubiquitous. These portable devices are held against people's brains, inserted into their ears, and sit in back or front pockets next to their reproductive organs. Where is all this leading us? Have we even asked? That person talking on her cell phone next to you is not only annoying because she is blasting her conversation into your space, she is also irradiating it. Is this any different than puffing on a cigarette beside you? We have removed tobacco smoke from our public places and let in cell phones. Have we considered the consequences with enough balance and seriousness?

The electromagnetic frequencies of Earth, humans, and other species on the planet are in the very low frequency and extra-low frequency ranges: 0-100 Hz. Brain frequencies, cellular metabolism, and heart frequencies match the frequencies of Earth. They are *resonant* with them. Previously, these ranges were believed to be too weak to have any substantial or meaningful effect on each other. But now that we understand *amplification* (the ability of systems with "stored energy" to take weak signals and increase the signal by as much as a million-fold) we know this to be incorrect. We are *sensing* fields and we are *responding*.

Could it be that after the "fallout" of the nuclear horrors of the postmodern world, we have been seduced into the assumption that more subtle forms of radiation are not dangerous? In fact, the "safety" level for radiation of any kind is still determined by measurements of "heat and thermal effects" established during that time period. This is misguided. As we have seen through the responses of the pineal gland and hippocampus, many subtle electromagnetic interactions not detected through the current "heat standards" are known to interact with and disrupt the innate *coherence* of life systems.

Unfortunately, these claims are easily disputed. Tests can be manipulated because there are many extenuating circumstances and varied environmental factors that play a role. A person is never exposed to only one field. There are always varieties mixing together in the atmosphere around us.

Coherence

Bio-Physicist Mae-Wan Ho informs us that all life is liquid crystalline.[70] This is a new finding, one that is hard for us to comprehend. How could we believe that we are liquid crystals? A crystal is matter in which the atoms are in an ordered, repeating pattern that extends in all three spatial dimensions. Crystals have long been used in electronics to *amplify* wave transmissions. Because of their *coherently* arranged pattern of atoms, crystals are exquisitely responsive. Now cutting-edge, scientific research is proving that all of life, including human life, is liquid crystals. The liquid crystal state is one between liquid and solid, a "mesophase," which is a *tunable responsive system*. Humans and life are *tunable responsive systems*. Liquid crystalline systems respond and tune themselves to electromagnetic messages in the environment. They can do this because they are *coherent*.

From quantum physics, *quantum coherence* is the way physicists describe the ability of quantum particles to be in touch with each other at very far distances, and though separated by space and time, to act as a unified whole. Quantum particles displaying *coherence,* though they appear to be separated, are able to communicate and respond instantaneously to messages and incoming information with no measurable time lapse and without traversing intervening space.

Coherence is a wholeness, a oneness, a unity that exists outside the usual limitations of space and time. Mae-Wan Ho states, "Quantum coherence does not mean that everybody or every element of the system must be doing the same thing all the time, it is more akin to a grand ballet, or better yet, a very large jazz band where everyone is doing his or her own thing while being perfectly in step and in tune with the whole."[71]

Dr. Ho asserts that the phenomenon of *coherence* exists in organisms at the macrophase level (larger than the quantum, micro realm) as well. This includes humans, animals, plants, and planets. *Coherence* is a biological reality. The bottom line: We are quantum beings. The quantum realm is not disconnected from us, it is not some disembodied realm *out there* or *under there* that is fascinating but separate. It is not just a "scientific discovery." It is the actual matrix of our being, of life, of the Universe.

Life is a series of nested *coherent* systems, from the quantum level up, which creates more nested systems of *coherence.* Particles like protons, which are made up of smaller particles called quarks, make up atoms, and atoms make up molecules, which in turn make up cells. Cells learned, through evolution, how to store energy. Stored energy is also *coherent* energy. In fact, macroscopic life is stored energy. The whole Earth is stored energy.

The electromagnetic waves created by our bodies are at the extremely low level of the frequency spectrum, yet because our bodies are *coherent*, they have the ability to *amplify* these waves, as well as waves encountered in the environment, in very meaningful ways—ways similar to what we saw previously in the description of the photon and the retina.

Mae-Wan Ho is not the only one identifying *coherence* as an integral function in the overall process of living organisms. Recently, scientists at Berkeley Lab have been able to empirically detect *coherence* at work in plants. Photosynthesis—a plant's ability to capture photons from the sun and transform them into green food for the plant to use later (stored energy)—is now proven to be a *coherent* event. The photon captured by the chlorophyll molecule creates a *resonance* through the cells of the plant. The cells in turn *amplify* the photon into an instantaneous *coherent* conversion. Now the solar energy is transmuted into chemical energy throughout the plant.[72] This all happens in what is called a femtosecond, which is 10^{-15} of a second.

The single photon's *amplification* in the photosynthetic process displays *coherence* at work. The plant is *coherent* at the macrophase level. The chlorophyll molecule has evolved a sensitivity to—an "intimacy" with—the photonic field of the sun. It is in *resonance* with it. This highly developed, acquired sensitivity has led to more complex organisms, which thrive on photosynthetic life.

The nested systems of *coherence* exist from the micro level up into the macro level, from atoms to plants, humans to trees, planets, and theoretically the solar system, the galaxy, and the Universe at large. It is important to remember that the *coherent* system is exquisitely tuned to and able to *amplify* electromagnetic messages in the environment, both naturally occurring and human created.

A Circuitous, Nonlinear Affair

Earth took 4.5 billion years to form the delicately balanced, interrelated systems that work together to maintain homeostasis in the human body. These systems evolved within the context of the electromagnetic environment of Earth. The hippocampus and endocrine system are extremely receptive to electromagnetism. They are designed to listen for the electromagnetic messages and transfer them to the rest of the body.

Each individual will react differently to electromagnetic "smog," depending on exposure, overall well-being, and levels of stress or happiness. Our body's responses to electromagnetic pollution are circuitous, not a clear, linear path of cause and effect. If the pineal gland is the master gland of the endocrine system, and its function is compromised, this could lead to a cascade of abnormal hormone production.

Communication runs amok. The body gets a bad or mistranslated signal from an unknown source and reacts, setting off a chain reaction, the end result looking nothing like the original communication. It is rather like a game of telephone played among children, where the ending sentence is far removed and unrecognizable from the original sentence uttered into the first child's ear. If, however, we can finally appreciate that our *coherent* bodies are reacting electronically to the electronic messages they are receiving, and *amplifying* these messages in ways never before imagined, this may offer us a better understanding of how to work with this energy safely.

Works Cited

Altman, Lawrence K. "Alzheimer's Disease Linked to Damaged Areas of Brain." *New York Times* 7 Sept. 1984.

Angier, Natalie. *Woman: An Intimate Geography.* Boston: Houghton Mifflin, 1999.

Ausubel, Ken. *Restoring the Earth: Visionary Solutions from the Bioneers.* Tiburon, CA: H J Kramer, 1997.

Becker, Robert O., and Gary Selden. *The Body Electric: Electromagnetism and the Foundation of Life.* New York: Morrow, 1985.

Becker, Robert O. *Crosscurrents: The Perils of Electropollution, The Promise of Electromedicine.* New York: Penguin, 1990.

Belokrinitskii, V. S. "Destructive and Repair Processes in the Hippocampus after Prolonged Exposure to Nonionizing Microwave Radiation." *Bulletin of Experimental Biology and Medicine Bull Exp Biol Med* 93.3 (1982): 337-40.

Cameron, D. O. *Symbols of Birth and Death in the Neolithic Era.* London: Kenyon-Deane, 1981.

Cohen, Elizabeth. "Antidepressants Most Prescribed Drugs in U.S." *CNN.* CDC, July 2007. Web. 08 Nov. 2010. <http://www.cnn.net/>.

Devereux, Paul, John Steele, and David Kubrin. *Earthmind: A Modern Adventure in Ancient Wisdom.* New York: Harper and Row, 1989.

Devereux, Paul. *Shamanism and the Mystery Lines: Ley Lines, Spirit Paths, Shape-shifting & Out-of-body Travel*. St. Paul, MN: Llewellyn Publications, 1993.

Dyer, Owen. "Alzheimer's Surges Unchecked." *National Review of Medicine* 4.12 (2007).

Eakins, Pamela, and Brian Swimme. *The Lightning Papers*. Unpublished Manuscript, 2007.

Ellis, Normandi. *Dreams of Isis: A Woman's Spiritual Sojourn*. Wheaton, IL, U.S.A.: Quest /Theosophical Pub. House, 1995.

Gimbutas, Marija Alseikaite. *The Goddesses and Gods of Old Europe 6500 to 3500 BC: Myths and Cult Images*. Berkeley: U of California, 1982.

Gimbutas, Marija. *The Language of the Goddess: Unearthing the Hidden Symbols of Western Civilization*. San Francisco: Harper & Row, 1989.

Grimassi, Raven. *Old World Witchcraft*. Weiser, 2011.

Ho, Mae-Wan. *The Rainbow and the Worm: The Physics of Organisms*. Singapore: World Scientific, 1998.

Ho, Mae-Wan. "Bioenergetics & Biocommunication." *www.ratical.org*. Mar. 2008. Web. Feb. 2010. <www.ratical.org/co-globalize/Mae-Wan-Ho/biocam 95.htm>

Kingsley, Peter. *In the Dark Places of Wisdom*. Inverness, CA: Golden Sufi Center, 1999.

Lentz, Carola. *Land, Mobility, and Belonging in West Africa*. Indiana University Press, 2013.

148

Meyerowitz, Eva L. R. *The Sacred State of the Akan*. London: Faber and Faber, 1951.

Northrup, Christiane. *Women's Bodies, Women's Wisdom: Creating Physical and Emotional Health and Healing*. New York: Bantam, 1998.

Sahtouris, Elisabet. *Earthdance: Living Systems in Evolution*. Lincoln, NE: IUniverse.com, 2000.

Salford, Leif G., Arne E. Brun, Jacob L. Eberhardt, Lars Malmgren, and Bertil R. R. Persson. "Nerve Cell Damage in Mammalian Brain after Exposure to Microwaves from GSM Mobile Phones." *Environ Health Perspect. Environmental Health Perspectives* 111.7 (2003): 881-83. Web.

Sarris, Greg. "Pomo Heritage Week." Sebastopol Community Center, Sebastopol, California. Feb. 2012. Lecture.

Schwenk, Theodor. *Sensitive Chaos: The Creation of Flowing Forms in Water and Air*. New York: Schocken, 1976.

Sofaer, A., V. Zinser, and R. M. Sinclair. "A Unique Solar Marking Construct." *Science* 206.4416 (1979): 283-91. Web.

Sterling, Ron, M.D. "How Stress Produces Major Depressive Disorder." *www.MindMatters.ws*. 12 Dec. 2006. Web. <www.MindMatters.ws>.

Swimme, Brian. *The Powers of the Universe*. The Center for the Story of the Universe & California Institute of Integral Studies, 2004. DVD.

Swimme, Brian, and Thomas Berry. *The Universe Story: From the Primordial Flaring Forth to the Ecozoic Era – A Celebration of the Unfolding of the Cosmos*. San Francisco, CA: HarperSanFrancisco, 1992.

Swimme, Brian, Perf. *Workshop on Race and Cosmology.* *http://www.caroline-webb-.com/Video.htm.* 5 June 2005. Web. Mar. 2012.

Tengan, Alexis B. *Hoe Farming and Social Relations among the Dagara of Northwest Ghana and Southwestern Burkina Faso.* Frankfurt: Peter Lang, 2000.

Walker, Barbara G. *The Women's Encyclopedia of Myths and Secrets.* San Francisco: Harper. 1986.

Yarris, Lynn. "New Quantum Secrets of Photosynthesis." *Science @ Berkeley Lab.* Sept. 2007. Web. Feb. 2010. <http://www.lbl.gov.Science-Articles/Archives/sabl/2007/Jul/quantumSecrets.html>.

Endnotes

1 Information received by me in a group divination.

2 Conversation with my original mentor in the Dagara tradition.

3 Carola Lentz, *Land, Mobility, and Belonging in West Africa: Natives and Strangers* (Indiana Univ. Press, 2013).

4 Notes from a retreat, *Powers of the Cosmos*, Santa Sabina Center, San Rafael, CA, October 2002.

5 Video clip, *Workshop on Race and Cosmology*, Sophia Institute, Holy Names College, Oakland CA, June 2005. *http://www.caroline-webb.com/Video.htm*

6 Raven Grimassi, *Old World Witchcraft* (Weiser Books, 2011), 94.

7 Eva Meyerowitz, *The Sacred State of Akan* (Faber & Faber, London. 1951), 70.

8 Alexis B. Tengan, *Hoe-Farming and Social Relations among the Dagara of Northwest Ghana and Southwestern Burkina Faso* (Frankfurt: Peter Lang Publishers. 2000), 76.

9 Ibid.,314.

10 Conversation with my original mentor in the Dagara tradition.

11 Ibid.

12 The information on objectivity was given to me in conversation on this topic by Lisa Z. Lindahl. See: http://www.lisazlindahlonbeauty.com/

13 Kenny Ausubel, *Restoring the Earth: Visionary Solutions from the Bioneers* (Tiburon, CA: H.J. Kramer.1997), 219.

14 Marija Gimbutas, *The Language of the Goddess* (San Francisco: Harper & Row. 1989), 25.

15 Theodor Schwenk, *Sensitive Chaos: The Creation of Flowing Forms in Water and Air.* (London: Rudolf Steiner Press. 1965), 15.

16 Elisabet Sahtouris, *Earthdance: Living Systems in Evolution* (San Jose: iUniverse.com. 2000), 38.

17 World Resources Institute 2000: 106.

18 Schwenk,15.

19 Mae-Wan Ho, *The Rainbow and the Worm: The Physics of Organisms* (Singapore: World Scientific. 1998), 80.

20 Brian Swimme and Thomas Berry, *The Universe Story* (HarperSanFrancisco. 1992), 87.

21 Sahtouris. 254.

22 Gimbutas, 1989. 282.

23 Gimbutas, 1989. 279.

24 Ibid., 282.

25 Ibid., 295.

26 Anna Sofaer, Volker Zinser & Rolf M. Sinclair. 1979. *A Unique Solar Marking Construct.* Science 206: 283-291.

27 Gimbutas, 1989. 295.

28 Paul Devereux, *Shamanism and the Mystery Lines* (St Paul: Llewellyn. 1994), 165.

29 Meyerowitz, 1951. 72.

30 Peter Kingsley, *In the Dark Places of Wisdom* (Inverness, CA: Golden Sufi Center, 1999).

31 Meyerowitz, 1951. 180-182.

32 When one is initiated as a stick diviner in the Dagara tradition, she is given a kit with "pieces" (objects such as stones, small branches and shells) in it to use when she divines. These *pieces* not only represent but *are* in fact living entities and energies. A particular stone is Earth, another Mountain, an abalone shell is Water. Certain *pieces* are selected by the diviner's stick for the divination at hand. These are the beings

that are speaking to the person who is receiving the divination that day.

33 Tengan, 2000. 76.

34 Conversation with my original mentor in the Dagara tradition.

35 See citation # 32.

36 Conversation with my original mentor in the Dagara tradition.

37 Information received by me in a group divination.

38 Information about the Diamond Lakes of the Laguna de Santa Rosa before the Mexican and Europeans came from a talk given by Greg Sarris, Chairman of The Federated Indians of Graton Rancheria, in October 2010.

39 Images found in books by Marija Gimbutas, *The Language of the Goddess* (San Francisco: Harper & Row. 1989), and *The Goddesses and Gods of Old Europe* (Berkeley: University of CA. Press. 1982.

40 See my article: *The Archetype of the Womb: Part II, Womb Ovens* in Appendix A of this book.

41 See Christiane Northrup, *Women's Bodies, Women's Wisdom* (New York: Bantam. 1998) and Natalie Angier, *Woman: An Intimate Geography* (Boston: Houghton Mifflin. 1999).

42 See Robert O. Becker, *Crosscurrents: The Perils of Electropollution, The Promise of Electromedicine* (New York: Penguin. 1990).

43 See my article — *Electromagnetism: A Circuitous, Non-linear Affair*, in Appendix B of this book.

44 Notes from a retreat, *Powers of the Cosmos*, Santa Sabina Center, San Rafael, CA, October 2002.

45 D.O. Cameron, *Symbols of Birth and of Death in the Neolithic Era* (London: Kenyon-Deane, 1981).

46 Barbara G. Walker, *The Woman's Encyclopedia of Myths and Secrets* (HarperSanFrancisco, 1983), 180.

47 Normandi Ellis, *Dreams of Isis* (Illinois: Quest Books, 1995), 180.

48 Ibid., 179.

49 Marija Gimbutas, *The Goddesses and Gods of Old Europe* (Berkeley: University of California Press, 1982), p.34.

50 Ellis, 354.

51 Gimbutas, 1989. 148.

52 Ibid.

53 Gimbutas. 1982. 70.

54 Ibid., 73.

55 Pamela Eakins and Brian Swimme, *The Lightning Papers* (Unpublished manuscript, 2007), 2-26.

56 Robert O. Becker and Gary Selden, *The Body Electric: Electromagnetism and the Foundation of Life* (New York: William Morrow. 1985), 245.

57 Words like frequency, duration, vibration, oscillation, resonance arise when we speak of this. For clarity: *Frequency* is the speed, the number of times the wave arises per second in a repetitive charge situation. *Resonance* is when frequencies match. When they match they are inclined to have more of an effect. *Vibration* is something moving. *Duration* the length of time is lasts and then there is *oscillation*: moving at a regular speed or that which creates and responds to electromagnetism. *Fluctuation* is an irregular pattern

58 Becker & Selden, 249 and Ho. 1999, 137.

59 Becker, 1990. 277.

60 In some scientific circles there is intense debate around whether or not the speed of light is the fastest speed in the universe. However, for now, it is the accepted scientific fact.

61 Ho,1998. 92.

62 Brian Swimme, *The Powers of the Universe*, Disc 1, program 2, DVD (San Francisco, CA. The Center for the Story of the Universe & California Institute of Integral Studies, 2004).

63 Becker & Selden, 264.

64 Paul Devereux, John Steele and David Kubrin, *Earthmind* (New York: Harper & Row. 1989), 78.

65 Lawrence K. Altman, *"Alzheimer's Disease Linked to Damaged Areas of Brain,"* (New York Times, September 7, 1984) & Ron Sterling M.D., "How Stress Produces Major Depressive Disorder," (www.MindMatters.ws, Dec. 12, 2006).

66 Elizabeth Cohen, CDC: *"Antidepressants Most Prescribed Drugs in U.S.,"* (CNN.com July 2007).

67 Own Dyer, *"Alzheimer's Surges Unchecked,"* (National Review of Medicine, June 30, 2007, volume 4, no.12).

68 Leif G. Salford et al, *"Nerve Cell Damage in Mammalian Brain after Exposure to Microwaves from GSM Mobile Phones,"* (Environmental Health Perspectives, Volume 111, number 7, June 2003).

69 VS Belokrinitskiy, *"Destructive & Reparative Processes in Hippocampus with Long Term Exposure to Non Ionizing Radiation,"* (Effects of Non Ionizing Microwave Radiation, USSR Report, 1982).

70 Ho,1998.

71 Mae-Wan Ho, *"Bioenergetics & Biocommunication,"* (www.ratical.org/co-globalize/Mae-WanHo/biocam95.htm/ March 2008).

72 Lynn Yarris, *"New Quantum Secrets of Photosynthesis,"* Science@BerkelyLab (http://www.lbl.gov.Science-Articles/Archives/sabl/2007/Jul/quantumSecrets.html, September, 2007).

Made in the USA
Middletown, DE
18 March 2017